Furthering
My Education

Furthering
My Education

A MEMOIR

➤

William Corbett

$\mathcal{Z}$

ZOLAND BOOKS

Cambridge, Massachusetts

First edition published in 1997 by
Zoland Books, Inc.
384 Huron Avenue
Cambridge, Massachusetts 02138

FIRST EDITION

Book design by Boskydell Studio

Printed in the United States of America

04 03 02 01 00 99 98 97   8 7 6 5 4 3 2 1

This book is printed on acid-free paper, and its binding
materials have been chosen for strength and durability.

Library of Congress Cataloging-in-Publication Data
Corbett, William, 1942–
Furthering my education :
a memoir / William Corbett. — 1st ed.
p.   cm.
ISBN 0-944072-74-7 (alk. paper)
1. Corbett, William, 1942–   — Family.   2. Poets,
American — 20th century — Family relationships.
3. Fathers — United States — Biography.   4. Fathers
and sons — United States.   I. Title.
811'.54 — dc21   96-37563
[B]   CIP

*For Marni and Arden Corbett
and for Paul Auster*

It is only in isolate flecks that
something
is given off

No one
to witness
and adjust, no one to drive the car

— *William Carlos Williams*

"I HAVE GONE TO FURTHER MY EDUCATION." In 1965 my fifty-year-old father wrote these words, in a legible hand for once, on a green prescription form and tacked this to the locked door of his office in a Connecticut shopping mall. For those who knew some of the reasons for his going, there was a rueful humor in his words, a humor that was surely lost on his patients who read them in dumbfounded surprise.

My father published this epitaph on a Thursday, his day off, and by Saturday he was in Rome. This was his first stop on a three-month vacation that eventually carried him and Gloria, the woman he went with, to a new life in Baghdad. It would be months before most who read of my father's leaving on the front page of Trumbull's weekly paper would have any inkling that he went, in pursuit of his education, to Iraq.

They knew only that he had left without warning and were shocked and bewildered. My father was the only doctor a great many of these three thousand patients had ever had. Several were near going into labor and others had medical emergences of various kinds. When they turned to my father's family, they wanted more information than we could supply. Soon they discovered what we already knew, that my father would not return and that he had kept no records over the past three years of his practice.

After posting his epitaph my father drove his Chevrolet station wagon (his Cadillac Coupe de Ville had long since been sold to appease creditors) to his best friend's used car lot in Bridgeport. As Louis Kaye came from his office to speak with my father he had no idea he would never see him again. Nor did Louis know that the $7,000 he thought he held in his safe for my father was no longer there. My father had taken it months before and left in its place seven dollar bills.

Louis saw at once how agitated his friend was, how "not himself." He asked my father where he was going. My father pointed to Gloria's car, now pulling up to the lot. He told Louis he had left his wife and was driving to New Jersey to think things over at his brother Frank's. Louis saw the dark rings under his eyes, and the way his suit hung on him. He knew there were things my father wasn't telling him, but what could he do? Frustrated, angry and suspicious but true to his code that you did not press a friend about his business, Louis watched my father and the woman he did not know by name drive away.

After ten feet they stopped, and my father got halfway out of the car to yell back, "The keys are in it. Keep it, it's all yours." He motioned to the Chevrolet. Louis waved goodbye. When he tried to start the car, nothing. Damn! He struck the steering wheel. It was out of gas.

As my father and Gloria waited to board their flight for Europe, I was on a train from Boston to Bridgeport. My mother had summoned me after someone called her with news of the note on my father's office door. When she called she knew only that my father had fled but had no idea where or with whom. Before I reached Bridgeport she was to find out.

In the meantime my father called my Boston apartment

from the airport. He told my wife Beverly where he was, and when she urged him to call home he explained that he could not do that because he was about to leave for overseas. He promised to write and clarify everything. He assured Beverly that there was plenty of money to support my mother and that she knew exactly how she was to be provided for and where to sell the kidney dialysis machine and I knew all this as well because I would certainly remember how we had gone over things. To Beverly's further entreaties he replied, "Things are not what they seem," and then he hung up the phone.

I took a taxi from the station to Louis's lot. When I walked into the office he was on the phone. Hanging up he looked at me and shook his head. He had his habitual cigar in its plastic holder between his teeth. The color in his always red face heightened, and he nearly yelled at me, "Your father left with another woman!"

"How can you be sure?" I asked, incredulous.

My innocence was too much for him, and he unloaded on me. "Because I tell you so. Because I know what in hell I'm talking about! Because —"

"My mother didn't say a —"

"Your mother didn't know. She does now. Oh, for Christ's sake don't look at me like that. You've got to grow up. You graduated college didn't you? You're married. You understand what I said. It's not the way I want it. It's the way it is."

I don't think Louis meant to humiliate me, but this is the effect his outburst had. More bewildered than when I arrived I shut up. The phone rang, and Louis answered it, grunting a few times before he got into a conversation. I stepped outside into the lot and lit a cigarette under the flapping plastic pennants.

Another woman? I knew nothing except that only days before my father had lied to me at least once.

Sidney, an acquaintance of my father's and business partner of Louis's, leaned on a car smoking a cigar. We shook hands and watched the smoke we were both sending into the air.

"Do you know why the doc went with her?"

"No. Until Louis told me a minute ago I didn't even know there was a her. He told me he was going alone."

"She gave him a blow job," Sidney said with no more expression than he might have put into a remark about the weather.

"She what?"

"The doc left because she gave him a blow job. Some men . . . it's as simple as that."

PART I

Shortly before World War One my father's father avoided service in Emperor Franz Josef's army by trekking alone from Pecs in Hungary to Cherbourg, France. There he removed the gold coins his mother had sewn in the lining of his coat and used them to buy passage to America. Arriving at Ellis Island in New York my grandfather had his name Americanized by an Irish immigration officer. As Frank Corbett he made his way to Hungarian contacts in Shelton, Connecticut, where, by and by, he met his wife, from whom, after his death, I heard of his walk across Europe.

Pecs, Cherbourg, gold — she provided no other details. Perhaps she knew nothing of her husband's family or background. She never said a word about either. Nor did she speak of her husband's life in Shelton before they met, and she offered not the smallest crumb of information about their courtship or the early years of their marriage.

Frank made a good living selling insurance to fellow Hungarians who knew English less well than he did. My grandmother dismissed his clients as "ignorant peasants," spitting out this phrase in Hungarian, a harsh sound in an otherwise melodious language. Frank did well enough to leave her four houses, divided into apartments, on the income of which she supported herself and her yearly winter cruises. Within weeks of my father's leaving she sold these properties and disappeared into Florida.

She kept only one photograph of her husband, which hung on her bedroom wall. In it he wore an old-fashioned two-piece bathing suit and sat at the top of a flight of stone steps leading down to a beach. My grandmother sat to one side of him, and to the other sat my grandmother's best friend. I was in my teens when my mother (source of nearly all that I know about my grandmother) told me, "Ma Corbett came home one afternoon to find that woman in bed with your grandfather. She never talked to her again."

My mustachioed, round-faced grandfather was built like a fireplug with a pouter pigeon's out-thrust chest. In my lone memory of him, he stands in our kitchen eating a piece of pie from a pie plate he holds up under his chin. He laughs and speaks a compliment, I think, to my mother, who has baked the pie. He could, my father liked to recall, turn the charm on and off like a faucet.

He died young, in his fifties, of cancer, an illness that was detected after he hurt himself falling on the ice when leaving the house of his mistress. He had moved in with this woman after my grandmother, on catching him in yet another infidelity, left him to "visit" relatives in Texas, where she was when he died. No one knew exactly where these relatives lived, so efforts to find her proved initially futile, and the funeral had to be delayed. When she eventually returned, only the family stood at the graveside. Returning from the service, my grandmother began to whimper, causing Frank, Jr., to curse her and order her to stop the tears, a scene that my mother several times acted out for me melodramatically.

My father told only two stories about his father. Shelton's only large factory produced sponge rubber. At some point the company prospered by turning out ice buckets. It also turned out a nasty, burnt rubber odor that hung over the town. A smell, my father joked, that would be sweet as flowers to us had his father bought into the company for the paltry $2,000 asked of him during the Depression. He had the money, according to my father, but missed his chance, and ours, at wealth because he feared the risk. A risk, my father implied, imagining *our* buckets rolling off the assembly line, he would have leapt to take on.

The other story got told at nearly every Sunday lunch we ate at the table in my grandmother's tiny kitchen. Her menu never varied — stuffed cabbages, chicken paprikash, noodles, green beans in a thin tomato sauce and for dessert hard, apricot-filled pastries dusted with powdered sugar. The heat from her stove made the cramped kitchen desertlike, and the sweat fell from us as we ate the heavy food until we groaned.

As the platter of stuffed cabbages came to the table, my father remembered his father's staying away from home on business for two or three days at a time. When he returned he went straight to his armchair in the living room, kicked off his shoes, loosened his tie and had a long and loud snooze. He awoke powerfully hungry and sat down, wordless, to the mountain of cold stuffed cabbages his wife had laid out for him. He polished off twenty-five of these, thirty if really hungry. After he had his fill he was ready to talk and reenter the life of his family.

At least I imagine he became active in the life of his household, but I do not know this for a fact. My father gave no hint of the role his father played in the family or in his growing up. He told no anecdotes of punishment or praise nor did he recount a household catastrophe or reminisce about a family outing. Nothing funny ever seemed to have happened in my father's family nor did he remember a characteristic gesture of his father's or any oft-repeated words of advice. The charm my grandfather was said to possess was left undetailed, and we saw only a gruff, imperious, silent old country businessman with an enormous appetite for stuffed cabbages. If my father read anything into this picture he kept those thoughts to himself.

All families keep secrets. My grandfather's philandering was one, but he stayed away from home on "business" for reasons other than skirt chasing. When I was twelve or thirteen, and my mother and I were at our closest, she told me something of my grandmother's role in what she described as a miserable marriage. She had never forgiven Pa Corbett for sleeping with her best friend, and over the years a frosty, uncomfortable truce had developed. They had hardly a word to say to each other, and you could cut the tension between them with a knife. No wonder the man didn't want to come home.

During those years my mother and I spent a great deal of time alone in her car. We lived in the suburbs, and I had to be driven to parties, Little League baseball games and dancing school. As she ferried me from place to place I heard her version of our family history. Not that I thought of what she told me as a version. I accepted her words as gospel and did not tire of her repeating them.

I already knew that my mother loathed my grandmother. I could see this loathing peek out from beneath the exaggerated politeness with which she treated her, and I heard it, full voice, when she told me anything about my grandmother. My mother's tales had the effect of enlisting me to her point of view, and I admit I never lost an opportunity to let her know I was on her side against the woman who insulted her cooking, never lifted a finger and had made life difficult for her since the day they met.

My grandmother's disappearance into Texas shortly before her husband's death had not been the only time she left him. Six months or so after the birth of Frank, Jr., my grandfather came home from work to a dark house. The next-door neighbor crossed over to tell him that his wife and baby were gone. Someone came by to deliver the message that they were on their way to Hungary. My grandmother had not even left her husband a note.

My mother had it from my father that my grandmother stayed "over there" for a few months before she left Frank with relatives and returned to her marriage. My father's birth less than a year later put the marriage on a new and, for a time, more secure footing. He was three or four when the brother he had never been told about arrived from Hungary speaking only Hungarian.

In telling this tale my mother milked it for all it was worth. Imagine, she practically hissed, a mother abandoning her infant son, her firstborn, in a distant land to the care of strangers. My father must have told my mother the gist of this story, but he lacked her feel for drama. Since she spoke every melodramatic word with total conviction, it may never have dawned on her that my grandmother's fabled flight is, at the least, improbable. My father was born in 1915, two years after his brother Frank. This means that Frank had to have been taken to Hungry around the time World War I began, in 1914. Such a journey had to have been both arduous and expensive. My guess is that my mother, no respecter of facts when she knew the truth, added Hungary (a dash of paprika), its distance from America emphasizing my grandmother's heartless neglect of her child, to actual events. But if this were true why did my father accept my mother's account as offered?

I was never to hear a word about these events from my grandmother. She slammed the door on her past, at least when speaking English. What past she kept alive while speaking Hungarian with my father I have no way of knowing, but what I know of her Hungarian background is even sketchier than what I know of her husband's. She proudly pointed to her high cheekbones and yellowish skin as evidence that she had Mongol blood and thus that her forebears had been original Magyars who had fought the Khan's Golden Horde. She said she was the daughter of an innkeeper, and so winning as a child that a visiting duke bounced her on his knee.

She never spoke of brothers or sisters nor did she describe her parents. Occasionally, I spent as long as a week at her apartment, but I never met a friend of hers. She belonged to no bridge club nor did she drive a car. She walked to her shopping, and when she dealt with the butcher and the Italian who ran the grocery she kept her nose high in the air. On the wall of her living room hung the photograph of a bearded man. It had been clipped from a Hungarian newspaper. After she heard that I had written my first poems, she identified this man as her relative who had once been Hungary's poet laureate.

As a widow, my grandmother took pleasure in long cruises each winter, from which she returned laden like a caravan camel with tourist junk: flimsy bows and crooked arrows from Ecuador, alpaca caps with earflaps from Peru, Haitian carved and garishly painted standing drums, a brass coffee table and ewer from Beirut, ebony African statues, curved Turkish slippers and jeweled daggers and llama rugs to be marveled at and displayed in our living room before being hauled to the attic and forgotten. Invariably, she also returned with a marriage proposal for which, also invariably, she had contempt.

A Haitian professor romanced her at an exclusive hotel, but he was a "black nigger." The captain of a boat she traveled on proposed, but he was interested only in her money. Where he got the idea she had money she did not say. A retired executive who wined and dined her before popping the question was too old and wanted a nursemaid! Hah, she snorted, and laughed in telling of the lengths these men went to in the hope of winning her hand.

She did return from one trip to Texas with a husband, George. A total surprise. She simply presented him at one of her Sunday lunches. They had met and married. What more needed to be said? My father questioned her in Hungarian, but he never said what, if anything, he learned. George smiled, and after lunch he sat outside in a lawn chair and talked a blue streak between puffs on his fat cigar. Later we all agreed that we had no idea what he was talking about.

By September George had been sent back to Texas, and before Christmas my father brought the news that my grandmother had been granted a divorce. After this George went unmentioned and, perhaps, unremembered except by my mother. In response to another of my grandmother's slights, a plate of her food barely touched or uncomplimentary words about a new dress, my mother gleefully got a rise out of my father by asking if he knew what had become of George.

As my grandmother aged she lost her interest in cruise ships and wanted to go on longer voyages to more exotic ports. She began to take freighters. When she turned sixty-five, she could no longer travel on these boats because they offered only rudimentary medical care if any at all. Unless, that is, she had a letter from her doctor. My father provided this, but foreseeing more problems my grandmother simply applied for a new passport and gave her age as sixty.

When my father had run through banks, friends, patients and a Hungarian credit union; when he had cashed in his insurance, mortgaged our home to the hilt and stripped the last savings account of the few thousand he had squirreled away; when the sheriff began to deliver a summons to our door every day, my father turned to his mother. She mortgaged the four houses she owned to raise the money he needed. There had never been any question that my father was her favorite. This help went for nothing, good money after bad, and then my father was on his way to loan sharks.

At the time I knew little of this. When my father's fortunes had unraveled to this point I was newly married and living in Boston. Indeed, after leaving home in October 1964 I never saw my grandmother again. In my last memory of her she wore a pink suit and pink pillbox hat at my wedding. She had often promised her houses, fifty-fifty, to me and my brother. We dutifully thanked her without believing for a second that this sour and hardy woman would ever actually die. When my father described her life force he shrugged. "Your grandmother? She'll piss on all our graves."

My father and I share the name William Tihamer Corbett. Growing up I was "Little Bill" to my father's "Big Bill." Tihamer (Tee*ha*-may) is Hungarian and of no origin significant enough to have been passed on to me. My father's mother chose William for its pleasing American sound, yet all her life she pronounced *W* as *V* and for Bill she said "Beel."

Although he admitted the year of his birth, my father did not believe in birthdays, and we never celebrated his. Birthdays, he told me when I was young, are for children.

He spoke almost not at all about his own childhood and adolescence, yet my father did not encourage an air of mystery about his growing up. He simply emphasized that his life began in medical school. For as long as he could remember becoming a doctor had been his dream, his calling. The other events of childhood were to him incidental and unremarkable.

Still, fragments of that childhood inevitably came to light. On the wall of his mother's apartment hung a sepia-toned photograph of my father, aged four or five, dressed in a velvet Lord Fauntleroy suit. His long curls fell to a wide lace collar. He remembered getting beaten up when he went like that to first grade. He also remembered working as a teenager at an after-school job in a gas station. A brand-new touring car pulled up to the pumps. While my father filled its tank a man wearing spats and a camel's hair coat got out of the back and stood making small talk about the weather. He paid for the gas and, folding a five-dollar bill the long way, gave it to my father as a tip. That man was, the mechanic said, the gangster Dutch Schultz.

My father liked to say that in high school he majored in girls and minored in dancing at Pleasure Beach in nearby Bridgeport. He winked away the details, leaving his rakish exploits to our imagination. By his senior year scarlet fever had left him bald, and he had grown the mustache he wore for as long as I knew him. Thus at eighteen, in a photograph taken on the day he left for college, my father was a thinner and less flamboyant (he would take to waxing the tips of his mustache into upraised points) version of his fifty-year-old self.

He proudly claimed he had not waited to graduate from high school but went, upon admission, to the University of Alabama. My father had been called to medicine, and he saw no reason to explain how he managed to enroll in one school without a necessary diploma. His brother, already a student at Alabama, was there to greet my father, who arrived with one suitcase wearing the indestructible sharkskin suit that would last for four years. In explaining why he and his brother went to college so far from home during the Depression, my father recited what he laughingly called the immigrant's motto, "Come Ellis Island, Go Alabama."

At the university he became engaged to a southern belle, a judge's daughter, until the disapproving judge sent him packing; befriended a roommate named Red Talmadge; saw the Crimson Tide football hero Tiger White swing his gorilla arms as he walked through the streets of Tuscaloosa and regularly visited a whorehouse where he was a favorite of the girls because he had "a cute way of getting on and off." He also heard Mel Allen, then Melvin Israels, broadcast Tide football games. Years later on a train home from Philadelphia after an Army-Navy game my father reminded me of this as we sat in the outer ring of a circle laughing as Allen told football stories.

According to my father, he did not need the formality of an Alabama diploma to enter Philadelphia's Hahnemann Medical School. His calling and brilliance seemed clear to all. His friend Red joined him, and they continued to room together. My father depicted Red as a grind while he breezed through his classes, rarely cracking a book. How had medicine come so easy to him? "Born to the stethoscope," he bragged.

Older looking because bald and mustachioed, and with an edge of arrogance in his manner, my father cut a dashing figure in the coffee shops and luncheonettes around the hospital where the interns and nurses hung out. At least my mother thought so. She had caught him giving her the once-over, and was impressed when he met her haughty stare with one of his own.

No one enjoyed being flirted with more than my mother. In her sixties she remarked on the men in restaurants who peered over their menus to take a gander at her. "No, not now, he's looking. . . . Now . . ." and I'd turn to see a man summoning the waiter. "Well," she preened, "it's no secret that for an old gal your mother still has a blouseful of goodies."

Both my parents remembered that my father had been giving her the eye throughout lunch on the day they met. On his way out of the luncheonette, my father strolled up to the table where she sat laughing with her fellow nurses, paused, drew on his freshly lit cigar, the very gesture, my mother thought to herself, of a sophisticated, mature man and, full of himself, used the old chestnut "Haven't I seen you around?" She claimed to have ignored this overture, but my father said this wasn't so.

My mother had come to Hahnemann from the small Pennsylvania railroad town of East Mauch Chunk. She decided on nursing after the Depression had forced my grandfather to withdraw her from Beaver College following her freshman year. My mother loved her time at Hahnemann and kept her yearbook close to her until her death. She even carried it in her car, binding disintegrated and pages loose, like an ID, and she never doubted the absolute truth of the words its editors had used to describe her at twenty-two: "stylish as next month's *Vogue,* changeable as the weather, funny as Disney at his best."

An only child, my mother had been nicknamed by an adoring grandmother "Gimmie–I want–Take me." She made all A's through school, traveled with her mother to Germany in the late nineteen twenties, modeled herself after Bette Davis and took up her lifelong smoking habit at sixteen. Once a coal miner's son, down from the hills for a dance, developed such a mad crush on her that he carved Pats, her nickname because she had been born on St. Patrick's Day, into his bicep with a jagged piece of slate. And once her father dragged her from the same dance floor. He had forbade her going, but she lied that she was visiting a friend and went to the dance anyway. Hearing from the neighborhood busybody that my mother was there, he marched up to the dance hall in the town park and without a word grabbed her by the arm, no matter how hard she cried or how embarrassed she was, and marched her back home.

My vulnerable, eager to be amused and to amuse mother did not enjoy the chase and soon let my father make his move. They quickly fell in love, at least she said that she did; I never heard him speak of their courtship. "All the Things You Are" became their song, and soon a justice of the peace married them.

The wedding took place before my father's graduation with neither family in attendance. Although they rushed things, my father, according to my mother, had reasons not to invite his parents. They had met my mother on a visit to Connecticut and had not approved of her or, at least, had given her the cold shoulder. She remembered going out of her way to win them over, but they spoke Hungarian during most of the visit, leaving her out — an act of rudeness that she swore never to forgive them for.

She liked to remind me that although she had ample reason to hate my father's parents she had kept on trying, had wanted to be a good daughter-in-law, but that they were impossible. At my father's graduation they all but ignored her again and did no more than say hello to her parents. She had never felt so . . . twenty years later she had no words for it. A slap in the face. Although never one to keep things to herself, my mother could say no more about this incident.

A possible explanation for their sudden marriage is that my mother was pregnant with me. My parents celebrated no set date for their wedding anniversary but preferred the spirit to move them sometime early each spring. I was born in October of my parents' first year of marriage, which means that my mother had to have been pregnant in February. Had we not gone to my father's Hahnemann class reunion the summer before I went to college, I might never have made this calculation. Going there made me focus on their past and put two and two together.

Of that trip I remember a large dissection hall empty save for its bare, platformlike tables, and a white-haired teacher who politely, and unconvincingly, said that of course he remembered teaching my father. It was in a cab on our way to lunch that my mother pointed to a window in an apartment building and whispered to me, "That's where you started." I understood this was a secret between us, and I nodded in response.

I was born October 11, 1942, in Norfolk, Virginia, a place of which I remember nothing. Within weeks of my birth my father had been shipped to the South Pacific, where he served throughout the war as a lieutenant commander and medic in the Navy. The adhesion that bonds parent to child, that inexplicable surge of love for your own flesh and blood that I felt so strongly when I first saw both my daughters, must not have taken between my father and me. Or this bond weakened during his years at war. When he returned he was not re-united with a son but introduced to a stranger, a little boy who had been raised by others and was now unwilling, in ways that he was unaware of, to let his father assert his father-hood.

Before he went to the war, my parents lived in a develop-ment of prefab houses with fellow officers and their wives, one of whom was my mother's best childhood friend, Lois Burcaw. Loie gave birth to her son Barry on the same day and in the same hospital where my mother was giving birth to me.

Life at Oakdale Farms, both before my birth and my fa-ther's departure and afterwards, was the best of times for my mother. She never said so directly, but early on I knew this to be true because of the jubilant way she talked about the place. My mother gave birth to me among women her age who were also having babies, their joy in motherhood intensified by the drama of their husbands going to war, at that point a new war, an adventure. Most had the concrete fact of a new-born, and the mystery, romance, fear and order of war. Life was both in their hands and totally out of their control. The few months at Oakdale Farms had, in my mother's recollec-tions, a texture and jam-packed density of incident to them that the dull days of three and a half years of war could only heighten.

My mother remembered a partylike atmosphere in which all the houses were open and everyone floated in and out of them. There were no plans to be made for the future except the most fantastic. Indeed, there could be no plans of a prac-tical nature until after the war, thus the present had their complete attention. The young men were equal in rank and status and equal before their unpredictable futures. There is a snapshot of my very pregnant mother posed in profile wearing a Nazi helmet and giving the Sieg Heil salute. In the background, houses, really not much more than flimsy beach shacks, sit tentatively on scruffy land that must have very recently been vacant. My mother's comic profile is imposed on an improvised world.

Then the men sailed to war. My father once began a sentence, "No man wants to leave his wife and baby son . . . ," but he left it unfinished, at least to me. In response to his friend Louis Kaye's ribald, hilarious account of his war in China, my father offered up a few anecdotes. He recalled lunch in an officers' mess with the touring Bob Hope and Hope's wildly mustached, googly-eyed second banana Jerry Colonna. He also told a complicated story about trading medical supplies to Australian pilots for bottles of scotch whiskey and how tricky the logistics of exchange had to be to avoid detection. These stories left me cold, so I invented a scene in which my medic father operated on wounded marines under flickering lights while the assault on Tarawa raged around him. I acted this out complete with the screams of the horribly wounded soldiers for my friend Johnny Stadler, whose older father had not been to war. I had, of course, seen that very scene in the movies and wanted those experiences for my close-mouthed father and myself.

In our attic, where my father's naval uniforms, summer whites to heavy bridge coat, hung in storage, I discovered large, canvas-bound scrapbooks of my father's war. Here soldiers stood calf deep in soupy mud, my thin, shirtless father among them. There were palm-roofed open-air rooms, grinning natives halfway up curving palm trees, wrecked jeeps, twisted forms that might have been burnt dead men and a soldier wheeling something huge and round in a wheelbarrow.

My father identified the soldier's burden as a testicle swollen by elephantiasis. I know I did not invent these books, but when, in prep school, I returned to look for them they were not there and my father had no interest in what had become of them.

Snapshots show that my mother's war, the early months of it at least, was child bound. I am bundled in a stroller, one in a flotilla of other bundled infants in strollers. I am on a blanket with other babies celebrating a birthday. In these pictures, chubby, happily laughing, healthy-appearing babies and laughing mothers look through the camera to their men overseas.

Before my mother and I decamped from Norfolk for her parents' East Mauch Chunk home, my grandmother Corbett paid what was to become a legendary week-long visit. The purpose of her visit was to see me, her first grandson, but, having looked me over, she paid no more attention to me, didn't want to hold me or change my diaper. Instead she expected to be waited on hand and foot. She offered no help at meals, never picked up so much as a dustrag to help clean nor could she bestir herself to walk to the corner grocery for a quart of milk. Oh, her queenly airs and the meanness and horror of that visit! And my mother's hands full with me! My mother's mother, who was not there, retold the story of it with a bitterness she sustained throughout her long life. It was one of the many grudges she held against that woman, and she needed little prompting to rise in righteous anger to its telling.

As she told me this tale she shook her head in wonder at my other grandmother's "devilment." We were in her East Mauch Chunk cellar, where she did the ironing on hot summer afternoons. After getting her going with an "innocent" question, I sat on the stairs, rapt. Her account had all the passion of their rivalry, of her absolute superiority and her desire to have me be *her* boy. I lapped up the attention, and swore to myself that I was on the right side, the Mench side. I had her tell the tale again and again so I could feel the glow of the warm bond between us.

But these sessions came later. When my mother returned with me to her parents' to wait out the war, I was an infant. The memories I have of the years before my father's return from war are for the most part not mine. If I can see myself at three split off from the procession of children parading down the main aisle of church and, waving my palm frond, march alone down a pew, only the palm showing, it is because I heard the story a dozen or more times. A story, incidentally, that was told to illustrate how it was my nature to show off.

What I do remember clearly is learning to read. My grand-father taught me out of self-defense. I can see myself, fresh from my evening bath, climb into his lap. I snuggle into the crook of his elbow and implore, "Read me, read me!" He puts down his newspaper and takes up a children's book. "Little Red Riding Hood," he begins and reads that story and then the three little pigs story. The following night I implore him again, and again he reads these stories. This goes on for many nights, until he teases me with "Little Green Riding Hood." "No, no, Poppy," I squeal and squirm in his lap. I grab for the book, brushing the pleasant roughness of his beard. "Do it right! Do it right!"

He enjoyed teasing me, and the rub-a-dub-dub of his big knuckles on my chest and skull that followed. I did too, but I really wanted to hear the story as I had heard it before. Soon I understood that I could hear the story for myself if I knew how to read. I began to pester my grandfather to listen to me as I haltingly read aloud the same stories I had memorized from his reading. Had my father returned by this time? He may have. I do know that after he did I continued my bed-time crawl into my grandfather's waiting lap.

Claude Mench, my grandfather, lived all of his seventy-five years in East Mauch Chunk. I loved him very much, more than anyone else in my family. He died when I was twenty, the first of my small family to go, and the only one to die while we still constituted a family. What I feel for him to-day remains pure, uncorrupted by the years since his death.

He spent all his working life as a clerk in the post office and left the hills of his birthplace, and their trout streams and lakes, as rarely as he could. He never drove a car or flew in an airplane. When his wife and daughter went to Europe he stayed home. He did go to Baltimore to visit his sister Isabel, only to return home the morning after arriving because she had served him cake on a dirty plate. The farthest he ever traveled from his home was, improbably, pre-Castro Cuba. That trip, by train to Florida and boat to Havana, he took to please my grandmother. Returning, he vowed never again, and his stubborn insistence on staying put became a family legend.

He loved to fish and to be with his men friends, but he never smoked, played cards or took more than an occasional social drink, though in a swanky New York restaurant he once ordered a Pink Lady. He stopped in at Milt Wietrich's barbershop every afternoon for the news and to gossip, voted straight Republican (he said he didn't care if a monkey ran on the ticket), hated FDR and invited not a soul into the living room of his own home. His fishing buddies called for him at the back door, and passersby, friends out for an evening stroll in summer, were entertained, if they had to be, on the front porch. He saw and talked with half the town every day at the post office, and the rest he encountered through his many good works.

As a young man he put an enormous amount of time and energy into laying out and constructing, wielding pick and shovel, the town park where my mother went dancing, and the diamonds where I spent large parts of my childhood summers learning baseball. He did this work without pay and, to hear my grandmother, without the thanks he deserved. He did not like her to go on about this and shushed her when she got started.

During the Great Depression he served as a town commissioner in charge of dispensing food to those on the dole. His hatred for FDR began there. Not because of anything Roosevelt did, but because my grandfather swore he had seen the flour he handed out dumped by the side of the road. He knew that those on the dole had done this, that what they had been given for free meant nothing to them. This waste infuriated him, and he reasoned that people will always be irresponsible with what they haven't worked for. He believed that Roosevelt's handouts encouraged this criminal irresponsibility, and with the evidence "clear as the nose on your face" he could not be argued out of this conviction.

After World War II he was one of the town fathers charged with restoring East Mauch Chunk and Mauch Chunk, which lay across the Lehigh River, to their prewar eminence as a railroad hub. This had been based on a switchback that rerouted trains, but shortly before the war it became obsolete and the Japanese bought the system. Since the war changed the nature of American transportation, there was no possibility of replacing the switchback, and the only hope for the town became an improbable plan to name it after Jim Thorpe, the great Sauk-Fox athlete who had recently died a ditchdigger in California. Thorpe's Pennsylvania connection had been with Carlisle Indian College down state from Mauch Chunk, where he had never set foot. My grandfather opposed the plan, but, when opposition collapsed, he threw himself behind it. The town put its hopes on a cancer hospital and research center (cancer was what had killed Thorpe) built from money donated by the Eagles fraternal order, a Jim Thorpe museum and the small business that would surely follow such development. In the end they got Thorpe's name and his corpse. The Eagles never came through, and the hospital proved a pipe dream. Litigation kept Thorpe's Olympic medals and trophies where they were, in Sweden.

My grandfather had more success in the Carbon County Fish and Game Authority, where he served in one capacity or another for nearly fifty years. All of these good works took him out of the house into a social world where he moved with considerable grace and good humor. He had the common touch and a word or joke for everyone he encountered. Before I was in my teens, he took me to meetings, and perhaps it was my love for him that I saw in others, but I felt him to be deeply cared for by his fellow townsmen. At home this "street angel" was a "house devil," a wicked tease (I have inherited this) and a man who pretty much did as he damn well pleased.

Around town my grandfather's nickname was Brocker, and by the time my father returned from overseas I was Little Brocker. If there was great excitement and anticipation before my father got off the train in his Navy whites, I remember nothing of it. I see him step from the train and walk through a cloud of steam toward me. I am told I ran to him, grabbing and hugging his knees, but I have no memory of this.

I now wonder at what point my father saw that I had become a Mench, more my grandparents' boy than his son. In the days after his flight to Baghdad my mother explained that he had left because of me, that the cause of his leaving went as far back as his return from the war to East Mauch Chunk. She knew that he felt closed out. He had never actually said so, but she knew it, and he never got over feeling that way. I resisted her theory. How could a four-year-old boy be responsible for his father's actions so many years later? With a dramatic gesture my mother waved me aside: I knew nothing of their world in 1945.

Now I can see there must be something to what she said. When my father met the family that had formed in his absence, he held back and failed to stake his claim to me. Soon he withdrew, however subtly, from his rights, duties and obligations. He wanted, I think, to be courted, but he wasn't, and the unspoken desires I assume he had went unrecognized until they hardened into an attitude my mother came only slowly to understand.

As a boy I read the blue-bound *World Book Encyclopedia* to put myself to sleep at night. I craved the names, dates and facts I found in the double columns of those volumes. Most of these stuck in my mind, helping to form the garbage memory, the Velcro memory I have today, to which the damnedest things will adhere. I may have a head full of assorted facts, yet as for most people, for me the dates of my family life, beyond births, graduations and deaths, have been lost in the living.

I do not know how long after his return my father began his search for a medical practice in Connecticut. We must have moved to Trumbull, than a rural town north of industrial Bridgeport, early in 1946. There he bought the practice of an elderly Yankee who dressed in a black three-piece suit and stiff-collared white shirt. I see him greeting my father and me, out on a house call, on the front porch of his white clapboard house. When I look closer this doctor becomes the actor Walter Huston. Anyone who writes an autobiography, I have to conclude, must own up to being an imaginative as well as reliable witness.

We moved into the first floor of Mrs. Smith's large Victorian house next to Zamary's Market on Trumbull's Main Street, and here my father hung out his shingle. In our front room he held office hours behind a folding screen. I remember lectures on how quiet I had to be during office hours, and I remember listening to the radio, turned low, as my father and his patients talked behind the screen. When in 1947, my brother Peter Craig, names of my mother's choosing, was born his crib stood in an alcove off this room. Peter had a pyloric spasm for the first year and a half of his life, and because of it spent long hours in that crib.

(Peter will appear so infrequently in this book that his relative absence needs to be explained. The five-year difference in our ages has something to do with this, but of more significance is that from the time I was six my parents sent me away every summer. Either I was in Pennsylvania with my Mench grandparents or I was, for one miserable summer, at camp. Essentially Peter and I spent our early years in two different families. Mine was with my grandparents and mother. Peter had my father and mother and, some of the time, me. Then I went away to prep school at thirteen and after that to college. That we grew up more apart than together and never developed the sort of relationship in which we confided in each other is reflected here.)

When we arrived in Trumbull it had just begun to grow

from a town of 4,000 into the bedroom community of 24,000 it became by the time my father left. The town sprawled, amalgamating four small hamlets. We lived in Long Hill, around whose modest green stood a grocery, dry cleaner and drugstore. There were several spare white Protestant churches in town, but the Catholic church, St. Teresa's, was by far the largest, and its congregation grew steadily as families arrived from Bridgeport.

The residents came to live in colonials, ranches, capes and Levittown-style houses in the developments going up on what had been farmers' fields. As my father drove over dirt roads to his house calls, he passed these houses that were inventing suburbia in postwar America. They had yet to become part of the landscape and sat awkwardly on their dirt yards. This must have been where he began to think of his town as real estate to be exploited and to muse upon his fortune coming from the exposed cement foundations and fresh blond skeletons of houses rising around him.

Not that he immediately plunged into house construction. Like many a returning veteran my father expected to reap the harvest he had fought to protect. He never stopped believing that his country owed him this, not just the opportunity but the eventuality. But first my father was a young doctor intent on building one of the two general practices in town, drawing patients to himself as much by his manner as by his skill.

While off-putting to some, my father's gruffness charmed many. He had a way of walking into patients' homes and ordering them around. He was especially good with older patients, the immigrant fathers and mothers whose successful children were now moving into suburban Trumbull. Addressing them in his few words of Italian, Polish or German, he put them at ease and they warmed to him. His take-charge air, beginning with a slight bow from the waist upon entering, gave both the sick and the well the comfort that help had arrived. My father *was* a know-it-all and did not like to be challenged let alone disagreed with even mildly, but this arrogance tended to enhance his authority. From the start he had the respect of his patients.

In his early thirties he began to shave his skull as the actor Yul Brynner would in *The King and I.* Then he let the ends of his mustache grow out and waxed these to curve up in points much as the artist Salvador Dalí had. No doctor in my father's set and certainly none of his lawyer or undertaker friends looked half so exotic as my father did. This might have led to his being thought eccentric, but somehow his appearance only added to his appeal.

He stood just under six feet tall and had an average build but small feet, size eight, and delicate hands. In the early years of his practice he favored racetrack suits, plaids and stripes, his taste, my mother kidded him, being all in his mouth. After I began prep school he abandoned his double-breasted loudness and his blue and forest green suede shoes for the sober black-vested suits of a preppie. He continued to wear bold, striped shirts, flamboyant for a professional man, and I remember a pair of heliotrope Bermuda shorts he sported in summer.

Not that he exhibited much of a sense of fun otherwise, at least not at home or around me. "I'll laugh when something's funny," he deadpanned, a natural straight man. Some thought him a stuffed shirt. He could go on without a trace of humor about the ferocity of our German shepherd Duke, my grandfather's running East Mauch Chunk from the barbershop, the nobility of our Magyar forebears or how little an appliance had cost wholesale. He liked to sit back in restaurants and give thumbnail diagnoses of people he had never seen before. That wheezing fat man had emphysema, that tall drink of water with the potbelly had an alcohol problem and that blond making her way across the room had to be a hooker.

For as long as I can remember, I heard my father characterized as a "moody Hungarian." This explained his being sunny one minute, dark the next, outgoing and then, at the flick of some inner switch, withdrawn and sullen. There did not have to be a triggering incident, at least not one that you could see. Suddenly dark, he became stolid, unbudging, his face set in an expression of expressionlessness, and he snapped out his displeasure. You had crossed some line that, a second ago, you did not know was there, some line that he would never reveal.

In the early years of his practice my father spent as much time in his car as he did at the office. House calls were his lifeblood, and he made them at any hour, day or night. He also served on the staffs of both Bridgeport hospitals, where he made rounds at least three times a week. From the start he drove large American cars, Buicks first, then Packards, and as he began to make big money in the midfifties he stepped up to Cadillacs. More car than he probably needed, he liked to admit, but he wanted, he explained, a helluva lot of metal in front of him in case he fell asleep at the wheel one night and had an accident.

My father's practice grew with Trumbull and prospered. Soon he had the money for a house to be built on Main Street from his design, a most eccentric design that produced large, awkward public spaces and cramped private ones. Our living room, for example, occupied one wing of the house but seemed added on as an afterthought. Having only a crawl space beneath it, the room held a chill for much of the year. As children my brother and I were forbidden to play in this room and reprimanded when we did. It had the stiff, formal air of a showroom, and the furniture stood so far apart, each piece seemed to be on display. Our large radio stood at the entrance to this room, and here I was allowed to lay on the carpet doing my homework while listening to Alan Freed's rock 'n' roll show from New York. After my father moved his office out of the house and replaced it with a "family room" complete with television, we entered our living room only on Christmas or for the big parties my mother liked to give.

At the other end of the house my father had designed a serpentine, crowded, impractical kitchen that my mother never ceased complaining about. There wasn't enough work space; the washing machine and dryer blocked cabinets; you had to move the kitchen table to get at the ironing board . . . The discomfort we all felt in this space must have contributed to the many fractious dinners we ate there.

Off the kitchen's working area, a bathroom led into my father's office. Since this could be used by patients, we and they were sometimes caught in an excuse-me-door-slamming farce.

Upstairs my brother and I had cell-like bedrooms. In dreams I am often back in my room, closed in between the dresser and the bookshelves that covered one wall. It is a claustrophobic sensation I cannot remember experiencing when I slept there. My brother's room had a door leading upstairs to the attic. Beyond that door a host of childhood fears lay in wait for him. Across the narrow hall was the large and rarely used guest bedroom. My father's walk-in closet ran along one wall. At night he hung his pants on that closet door. Mornings, before school, I often crept, holding my breath and heart racing, into this room to reach into his pants pocket and draw out a five- or ten-dollar bill. I wanted the money for candy bars and comic books, but the stealth and thievery itself thrilled me. If my father missed these bills he never let on. My mother once pulled a crumpled five-dollar bill from the pocket of my dirty dungarees. She suspected something, but I protected myself with a lie to her face.

About the time I went to prep school, 1956, my father had a swimming pool put in off the cement patio behind the living room. The contractor, a patient, gave him a deal. It was one of the first private pools in town, and the only one in our neighborhood of working people, whose houses were much more modest than our own. Beyond the pool, across an expanse of tall grass, stood a caved-in pigeon coop, an eyesore that eventually was torn down. Here my father attempted to raise show pigeons, but he quickly lost interest, and when he did, a plague of rats invaded the coop to attack the pigeons. He set traps. Through one fall we heard these go off at night like gunshots. Mornings he went out, followed by my mother's cries of revulsion and "please tear the goddamn thing down" to find fat dead rats. But the traps did not slow the invasion, and soon the rats deserted the coop and chewed their way into the cellar. More traps had to be set. Finally, a crisis having been reached, my father had a metal cellar door installed and got rid of the few bedraggled birds still left and with them my mother's morning ration of nagging.

So long as my father stuck to medicine, he did very well, but he repeatedly vowed that he had no intention of working all his life. He considered work of any kind, even the medicine he had been born to, a means to an end that he never defined. He had no hobbies nor did he outwardly harbor any fantasy interest, like sailing alone around the world, that he wished to pursue. He had no idea of what he wanted to do other than that it would be what he pleased, but he had a crystal-clear image of the fortune he would need to afford this freedom. He could have given it specific weight and volume and told you how tall it would stand in a corner or how much of his closet it would fill. Perhaps he counted on this fortune, once accumulated, to reveal his goal. In the absence of anything but the desire not to work, he did claim that all his efforts to make money were for us — "I'm doing this for your mother and you and Peter." We accepted this declaration at face value.

He worked hard and, within medicine, imaginatively. His single business success outside his practice came when he saw early on the need for convalescent homes. He went into partnership with a Bridgeport druggist, the only shrewd partner he was ever to have, and they built a hospitallike brick "home" in nearby Stratford. From the start this earned them both a handsome profit, and in the end it was my father's involvement in geriatrics that introduced him to Gloria, who managed several nursing homes.

My father could not be content with Stratford's success nor did he attempt to expand upon it. Instead he and his druggist partner planned to manufacture prescription drugs, a business that doctors were barred from for ethical if not, at the time, legal reasons. He and the druggist figured they had an angle. Whatever it was, it worked out for the druggist, but my father ran afoul of his colleagues. He fought their arguments, and when reprimanded felt unjustly singled out. He railed at the other doctors, some of them friends, whom he believed had cut him out of the pot of gold they themselves had dipped into on the sly. His mistake had been in being so bold about what he was doing, so frank and aboveboard. In this as in several other failed schemes my father blamed his essential honesty for his failure. He had not taken out a license to steal and wouldn't stoop to such a thing.

He next turned his attention to raising guinea pigs for sale to laboratories conducting medical experiments. This he did in company with a patient, a Welshman named Griffith Jones. After my father had cured Griffith of a persistent stomach complaint, the older and beautifully mannered man became devoted to him. Griffith's wife had died, leaving him to raise a foster child, Ray, alone. Griffith worked pumping gas at a service station on Main Street and lived on a run-down farm off a twisty road not too far from our house. On this farm stood a large, empty barn.

It was Griffith's idea to fill this barn with guinea pigs. He offered to let my father in as a favor and with my father's investment built cages to the rafters. Griffith and Ray would care for the pigs while my father used his medical contacts to place the pigs in research facilities, and out of this simple arrangement both would get a nice piece of change.

When my father and I were out on house calls, we often stopped in to inspect the operation. Griffith, enthusiastic and winningly sincere, and the sideburned, sullen Ray showed us around, even had us climb a tall ladder to look in on the scurrying pigs in the topmost cages. The only problem Griffith saw was how to dispose of the incredibly large quantity of "pellets" the animals produced. He didn't think it could be used as fertilizer, but, as it turned out, this wasn't a problem for long.

One afternoon a month and a half into the venture, Griffith called our home number. He was in a panic. He told me my father had to get out to the barn at once. When my father finished office hours, we drove right out. Griffith, his long face in tears, stood in the barn. As he talked excitedly his bushy eyebrows fluttered. The pigs had died sometime in the morning. Dead as doornails. Unbelievable. He had come to feed them and found every last one of them dead. He couldn't seem to believe what he was saying. He threw open a few cages to show us, and brought out pigs in both hands. My father stood stunned and held a still warm pig. No marks. No animal could have done this. No kids could have killed the pigs for a prank. We looked in several more cages, and saw more dead pigs on their sides. My father was as dumbstruck as Griffith. Ray and I climbed the ladder and found dead pigs in every cage, all the way to the top. When the vet came he quickly identified a respiratory disease, a kind of galloping pneumonia, as the killer.

My father lost no more than a thousand dollars in this misadventure, a loss he could easily shrug off. Had my mother seen the humor in this episode it might have become a family joke, but for her the dead pigs became a symbol of my father's folly and she derided him. Some businessman! He couldn't even keep a guinea pig alive! When other, and more costly ventures crashed, she brought up the pigs and berated him with them. He knew that their deaths weren't his fault and that she was unjust, and he argued with her, but she would not let up. Feeling misunderstood, he withdrew into silence. If he kept future plunges more and more to himself, he did so partly because he disliked my mother's sharp tongue, was no match for it, and also because he felt that if she could not stand behind him he would go his own way and show her. My mother, loving conflict, could never keep her mouth shut and always said more than she meant. My father, given to the drama of self-pity, clammed up.

The pigs had a second act when Ray befriended me. He was at least five years older, and I was flattered when he began coming over after school. I showed him through the house, from my father's antique gun collection in the attic to the run of *National Geographics* in the cellar, where there also stood a large safe, which, unbeknownst to me, my father did not keep locked. One night Ray walked into the house through our unlocked kitchen door and took from the safe the few hundred dollars my father kept there. He fled to New York City, I was told, where the police caught him, and soon he was sent to reform school. Griffith's abject apologies every time we stopped for gas had the effect of convincing me that I had been wrong to let Ray in the house and that the break-in had somehow been the result of my carelessness.

The night of the burglary my father had thought he heard something but had not bothered to investigate. He swore he would have wrung the little bastard's neck had he caught him. From now on the doors were to be locked, and my father bought a .45 automatic, which he kept in his bedside table against other mysterious noises in the night.

He recovered from the guinea pig venture and went into partnership with a jeweler, a patient and friend who bought estate jewelry, old-fashioned gawky pieces, cheap at auction. My father put up the money, and the jeweler removed the gems from their hideous Victorian settings, resetting them more simply to create several rings or pairs of earrings. The designs sold well, and my father made a profit, which he took in the form of a diamond ring for my mother. It was large as a knuckle duster. She loved it on sight and flaunted it until the day she died. She believed the ring to be worth a fortune, easily a college education for both my children. After her death my brother sold the ring through a fellow Hare Krishna for $3,000. He had been turned away by several jewelers, who showed him through the loupe that the diamonds were yellowish and only a grade above those used by industry, a fact I doubt our father had known.

My father's partner would also disappear from Trumbull with another woman. He did this within months of my father's leaving, so that some put two and two together and word got around to my mother that maybe the doc and the jeweler had been up to something together. She believed there was no way this could be true. At first she laughed, but then the gossip made her angry. It diminished her status as *the* woman scorned. Her trials were too fresh, and her need for comfort too great, for her to concede for a moment that another woman shared even the smallest aspect of her story.

From the beginning of their married household until my father abandoned it, my parents ran their economy on cash. Every Friday my father handed my mother new bills, $100 in 1948 and three or four times that much fifteen years later before his fortunes plummeted. This was hers to spend on food and domestic necessities, and because she liked to manage efficiently she was able to save money. Put money aside I should say because this savings did not go into the bank. My mother needed to hold and count her cash. She kept her nest egg in a handbag and might raid it to buy something special for herself even though it was my father's pleasure to give her whatever money she wanted for shopping trips. Until a year and a half before the end he was never less than lavish, and she always kept a little of this largesse for a rainy day.

My mother was a housewife who after our move to the Stonehouse Road house had "help," black ladies who rode the bus from Bridgeport, twice a week. She belonged to no clubs nor did she serve as a volunteer. She had neither charities nor causes. When my father joined the Algonquin Club, she bowled in their league. She was home when her kids came from school, and when her husband came in for dinner she had a meal prepared. Otherwise she relied on the two or three intense friendships she had going at any one time, but she was never really one of the girls.

In the early fifties she starred in several amateur theater productions. I can see her on a high school stage, teeth blackened, hands on hips, playing the owner of a junkyard in *Chicken Every Sunday*. She gave herself wholeheartedly to her parts. She even dragged my father into a bit role. When he strolled onstage in a drawing-room comedy and stood ready to deliver his lines, he was so obviously a fish out of water that his mere appearance brought down the house. Years later, while wistfully remembering the fun of these productions, my mother confessed to me that she had had an affair with one of her directors. She let this drop as if she were playing a part, wanting me to pick it up and question her, but, repelled by her theatrics, I merely nodded my head. If my father ever knew, and this had any impact on their marriage, she did not say, and I did not ask.

After my brother started grade school, and my mother learned to drive, she went shopping for clothes at least once a week and frequently more often. Alone if need be but usually with a friend, she drove to Bridgeport and then farther afield to the Post Road in Westport, where she might visit several dress shops. She came to enjoy the company of the women who ran them and their gossiping as much as the clothes she tried on. But she did love good clothes, and she loved a bargain. She brought home something from nearly every outing. Until the onset of menopause, which cruelly coincided with my father's failing fortunes, my mother seemed perfectly content with her life.

When she went out in Trumbull to the Grand Union for

groceries or on some errand, she liked to go in style. Ten years into his practice and doing very well, my father bought her a full-length mink coat. To own one had been her dream and his too. We went to a furrier's loft near Penn Station in New York City, where the salesman expertly tossed a coat to the floor and it flared and fanned out like a fur scallop shell. My mother liked to wear her mink over a pair of tight crimson toreador pants and a tight cashmere sweater with a mink collar and rhinestone buttons. She added her diamond ring to complete the outfit and drove in her sky blue Buick Roadmaster convertible to buy steaks for dinner. To push a cart down the aisles of the supermarket thus dressed to kill epitomized my mother's idea of class.

She loved that mink coat, and she loved the mink stole and jacket that followed it as my father's income and status rose. When his debts stripped these from her, she cursed his bad judgment and wept bitter tears. Her minks and her style were innocent victims, and she hated my father for taking them from her. Not that she would have used the word *hate.* "I loved your father" was the way she put it after he left, "but there's a lot I didn't like about him. Do you know what I mean? Do you know what it's like to love someone and dislike them at the same time?"

Like his domestic economy my father's practice ran on cash. Because house calls required him to make change, he carried a wad of bills in his pants pocket. It was from this that I peeled off the bills I stole from him. He usually carried a couple of hundred dollars in singles, fives and tens. In his wallet he carried larger bills and always a few hundreds or "C-notes." During his flush years he also carried several thousand-dollar bills. I heard him ask clerks if they had change for a thousand. Of course they did not, and, the bill already in his fingers, he had the delight, without letting his poker face betray his pleasure, of showing it to them.

The carrying of thousand-dollar bills may have been a form of identification in my father's set. An undertaker and his wife once came to spend the night of a big party. Just after arriving the undertaker went out to inspect our new swimming pool. He walked out onto the diving board. It had been unbolted for the winter, but the pool had not been drained. After a few steps the man fell into the icy water. In our kitchen, before he removed his soaked clothing he plucked a thin black wallet from his back pocket and asked for a cookie sheet. Helen, the maid who served at my parents' parties, brought it, and we watched as the man used thumb and forefinger to draw out a thousand-dollar bill. He spread it on the cookie sheet. Four more followed. He spread these on the sheet with the studied nonchalance of one who knows he is impressing his audience. He played his scene deadpan, then went upstairs to change into dry clothes. My father was a man of few anecdotes. This became one of them.

From the moment after my father left there were rumors that, far from going away broke, he had fled to the lifeline of a numbered Swiss bank account. If this is true it would have been the first time in his life that my father had ever saved money. I am sure, however, that he had at least a pocketful of cash. Even with the wolves at the door, he carried a large roll. The spring before he left I stopped in Trumbull on my way to New York with two friends. After a good dinner with plenty of wine, I asked my father if he could cash a check, one for me and one for my friend. "How much do you boys need?" He pulled from his pocket a fistful of bills, peeled two hundreds off the top and added a nice crisp fifty to mine. My friends and I were suitably impressed by the gesture.

I spent childhood summers with my Mench grandparents at 905 Center Street, East Mauch Chunk (later Jim Thorpe) nicknamed The Switzerland of America and county seat of Carbon County, Pennsylvania. I first went there, returning to what had been my home during the war, in 1947, the summer after my brother's birth. I continued to go until 1955, the summer before I started eighth grade, when I was packed off to summer camp.

Each June as the day to leave for Pennsylvania approached and my anticipation became nearly unbearable, I had the same nightmare. I dreamt that the summer had passed and with it the months I had spent at my grandparents'. I had been there but could not remember a single thing that I had done. Scared, heart pounding, I had to come fully awake to realize that it was a dream and the summer was yet to begin. Usually my mother drove me, and I stayed until Labor Day weekend.

As a child and into early adulthood I had no reason to question why I spent every summer away from home. In my thirties, after a series of anxiety attacks impelled me into a brief course of therapy, I began to see these summers in a new light. By this time I had children of my own and could not imagine being apart from them for the entire summer. Perhaps I had originally been sent to my grandparents' because of my brother's delicate stomach condition and the need to keep the house quiet around him. And after I'd spent a summer in Pennsylvania and loved it as much as I had, my parents did not have the heart to keep me from going again. Yet, as I thought things through, I saw that my grandparents were not to be denied. I had become their Little Brocker. I became convinced that my mother sent me to them because she could not say no to them. I'm sure my father had no objection to my going away. He must have looked forward to having his wife more to himself.

My grandparents loved me without limit, and though they doted on me they did not baby me. I had the run of their small town. I could not have enjoyed this freedom in suburban Connecticut, where the distance to swimming hole and baseball diamond kept a summer's day from evolving on its own. Nor were my parents disposed to let me go off by myself. During the school year I had orders to "report in." In Pennsylvania I went forth every morning from a snug harbor to enjoy whatever the day held. There I was twice blessed: I have not known such freedom and ease since.

A tall, thickly branched and full-leaved tree leaned over the street and sidewalk in front of my grandparents' house. It created a shadow whose cool density remains my measure of summer shade. The contrast between this shade and the bright sun into which I walked in the morning has become more intense in my memory as the years have passed. I see my grandmother sweeping her spotless front porch, raising a little night dust into shafts of sunlight. Nanny was a tireless housekeeper, whom my teasing grandfather compared to the bustling woman on the Dutch Cleanser can. During spring cleaning she even removed the mattresses from her beds in order to swab the bed slats with Renuzit. You could eat off her floors, she boasted, and the smell of her house, a perfume of paste wax, fresh air from the open windows, scouring powder and pine scent, defines clean for me.

She ironed the bedsheets we slept on, sheets that had dried on the line in her backyard, and these too gave off an odor of incomparable sweetness. I awoke in their comfort, ate a large breakfast topped off, as often as not, with a piece of molasses crumb pie and strolled out the door with my fielder's mitt looped through my belt. I mounted my bicycle and pedaled uphill to the town park, the one my grandfather had helped build, the one where my mother had played as a child and danced as a young girl. There were a half dozen swings, on which, standing, you could flex your knees, pumping yourself up until the chains rattled and you were thrilled to be nearly horizontal. There were seesaws, monkey bars, a merry-go-round, and there were also out-of-bounds places to explore. Bad boys, we crawled through a dark and narrow tunnel under the bingo hall and into the room where soda and beer were stored, testing and scaring the bejesus out of ourselves.

We slipped single file into the thick woods that surrounded the park and followed a path to the clearing where the Jolly Men's Club had their summer banquets. Here we sat at one of the long rows of picnic tables and rolled cigars from dead laurel leaves. We lit up with kitchen matches, drawing in the thick blue smoke until we choked and tears poured from our eyes. Here we swore like troopers for the sound of the forbidden words, salting our simplest sentence with sonofabitch-bastard, hell and damn.

But we lived to play baseball all day long on the diamonds across the cinder alley from the park. We always had enough boys for five against five, no hitting to right field, and often we were able to field nine-man teams. One of us spit on a flat piece of red stone and flipped it in the air while another called wet or dry. "Wet!" and sides were chosen. All of us had nicknames, so Connie Beans joined Harry the Left-hander, Whiskey and Pippi Rader; and the uncoordinated Butchie Eichorn got picked last. Except for my grandmother, everyone in town seemed to have a nickname.

Buck Rader, Pippi's older brother, came to play after work

and belted line drives that had us jumping. We had enough gloves to go around, cracked bats held together with screws and friction tape and two or three filthy balls softened up from use. We never kept score, and we played until, tired and thirsty, we rode our bikes to Frank Hoeing's housefront grocery, where we spent our nickels on cold soda and Popsicles.

There must have been rainy days, but I do not remember them. Terrific thunderstorms did come two or three times a summer, late on the afternoons of especially humid days. East Mauch Chunk is in a bowl formed by the small, rounded mountains that surround it. The sky might be blue directly above us when we heard thunder, then the storm clapped a black paw over the town and rain came down, in my grandfather's words, for which my grandmother shushed him, "like a cow pissing off a flat rock." Lightning cracked open the black sky. My grandfather knew a grown man who hid under his bed. Some townsfolk left their porches for indoors until the rain and noise let up. When the storm passed, my grandfather and I prowled carefully with a flashlight over the wet lawn in search of "wormies," night crawlers.

We put these in a coffee can, then dropped its contents into the dirt-filled worm box my grandfather kept under the back porch. When he needed worms for fishing, he lifted a handful from the writhing, tangled mass into his green, banana-shaped worm tin. He went fishing three or four times a week. As I got older I went out with him, in the afternoons to stream fish for trout and at night, for a special treat, to fish for catfish in Brady's Lake in the pine swamps an hour from home.

We drove out with the Young Fella, whose thirties touring car had no floorboards, or with the One Armed Fella, who steered with the stump of his missing arm when smoothly shifting gears, or with Puppy Armbrister and young Joey Angelovich, who worshiped my grandfather. When we fished streams we carried pails to fill with huckleberries. My grandfather reached up to pull down the high berry bushes so I could fill our buckets, picking the large, juicy berries with both hands. Out of the brimming pails we brought home, my grandmother baked pies and then froze the rest of the berries in their own syrup. The native trout (brookies) we brought home she fried for our dinner. The sweet, flour-white-fleshed catfish we ate for breakfast before, exhausted, we fell into bed and slept off our night at Brady's, where the moon had shone through a ruined mansion on the far hill's side like a jack-o'-lantern.

Idyllic? Absolutely. And so was every other night, whether I watched wrestling on TV in my freshly laundered pajamas or just sat on the front porch enjoying the lightning bugs and the conversations about nothing much that my grandparents had with friends out for a stroll. I did get in dutch for swearing, for playing in the fresh tar spread on our street and once for riding my bike downhill crossing three streets and the state highway before, failing to hold a left turn, I crashed into a dump of coal ash. I made this ride on a dare and had to be walked home, my bike wrecked. When my grandmother saw me, bloody-chested and ashen, she cried so that it brought neighbors out of their houses. She bathed me in the cellar's soapstone set tub and nursed my scrapes and cuts while, breathless, I recounted how scared I had been, so scared that I had shut my eyes.

But my only really bad moments in Pennsylvania came when my mother called to set the date for my return home. "It's not that I don't love my mommy and daddy"— I sat on the back porch sobbing into my grandmother's aproned lap — "it's just that I love you and Poppy more." I must have thought about my parents during those summers, missed something of home, but I cannot remember doing either. Back in Connecticut I sat in the cooling bathwater and cried my eyes out for my grandparents and Pennsylvania.

As my father's practice prospered, he spent his money as quickly as he made it, "hand over fist," my mother later complained. It was his idea to send me to an expensive boy's camp, Camp Idlewild, on an island in New Hampshire's Lake Winnipesaukee, for six weeks the summer before I entered eighth grade. I fought going, but cry and rant and rave as I might I could not sway my parents from doing this for me.

When I got to Idlewild it felt like prison. The counselors were guards who thought themselves lower in class than the inmates and therefore more noble. Under their control were the camp's many sons of rich South and Central American colonels whose footlockers bulged with candy and "skin" magazines and who carried cash in the pockets of their camp shorts. Among the other inmates were bed wetters, who were forced to stand holding their soaked and stinking bedclothes on a boulder outside the cabin where I slept. I hated the place, hated being away from Pennsylvania, hated myself for briefly falling for the camp line and competing for chevrons of excellence, hated the rifle range and the bullying counselors and senior boys. Finally, I ran away. Actually, rowed away.

Another boy and I discovered that you could take out a camp rowboat for an after-dinner row. We quickly realized that no one was watching to prevent our rowing out in the lake and across to the mainland, where we figured we could hitch rides home. No matter that home was hundreds of miles distant. We were both miserable, so we rowed and on our first attempt were caught within sight of the far shore. We promised never to pull that stunt again, and rewarded the counselors' trust with another break. This time they punished us by taking away our after-dinner candy privileges. Barred from the camp store, we bought our candy from a Guatamalan boy, a black marketeer and loan shark, and we plotted another escape. This time we took off before dinner and, aided by an unusually windless day, made it to the mainland and had our thumbs out when the camp speedboat *Riot* came with the gendarmes to corral us. This worked better than we could have hoped for. The camp director declared us incorrigible, and I was sent home, by bus to Boston and then by train, in disgrace. But the string of summers at my grandparents' had been broken, and I was never to return there for more than short visits.

On one of these visits during the next summer, when I was thirteen, I wrote my first poem. Since I had spent the previous summer at camp, I had been away from Jim Thorpe for nearly two years. After dinner on my first night I walked up to the deserted park, sat idly on one of the swings and then walked beside a shallow drainage ditch toward the empty baseball diamonds. Without warning, a voice inside my head spoke these words, "The gray sky sets on the gray hills/the town lives out its death." I knew at once that I had to write them down, and I walked quickly back to my grandparents' house to do so. I also knew that these words were the beginning of a poem, even though the only thing I knew for sure about poetry was that, unlike prose, it did not have to fill up the entire page. You could break the words into lines, and this I did while my grandparents and my mother looked on. I wrote with total unself-consciousness, and I can still feel the pencil in my fingers and the ribbed rattan mat on which I sprawled. Soon I had a ten- or twelve-line elegy, not that I knew that word for it then, and I passed it around. Instant approval! I had no idea I wanted to be a poet, but I knew within a few years that I did, knew even though I would remain ignorant for many years of what being a poet meant.

My grandmother kept that poem and without telling me took it to Joe Boyle, the editor of Jim Thorpe's weekly paper. Boyle did her the courtesy of reading it but said there was no place for it in his paper. My grandmother urged the poem on him. She could be a warrior where my mother or I was concerned, and she got it into her head that Boyle's response slighted me. He still said no, for which insolence, she proudly told me, she never said so much as how do you do to him again.

By the time I began to realize that half the time my father communicated with me through my mother, the pattern had been set. The peculiar feature of this pattern was that she gave me only his words of praise. I can't be certain how many of these my father actually said or wanted passed on or how much my mother invented in his name. Disappointments, dissatisfaction, anger and punishments he gave out firsthand. But if I did well in school or, later, in sports, or had accomplished anything of note, my father's reaction came through my mother.

The words of a go-between are often sweet, and for many years what my mother said made me feel good. But by prep school I knew a widening gulf stood between my father and myself. I had begun to doubt that he really cared for me. When he spoke at our football banquet (he served as the unofficial team doctor during games), he extolled in a few awkward phrases my play at linebacker as "the best" on the team.

I blushed with embarrassment. I knew I was not the best, and knowing this my father's words rang false. It certainly didn't sound like the praise my mother gave me in his name. I couldn't tell him that I thought him insincere, but this is what I felt.

He, too, recognized the distance between us, but in a way that implied he considered it no more than natural, the chasm that inevitably separates father from son. He quoted Mark Twain's observation about the fourteen-year-old son thinking his father stupid only to discover upon reaching twenty-one how much his father had learned. He added a personal twist to this by interpreting the boy's attitude as ingratitude. To him Twain's remark did not chuckle over a callow son but condemned an ungrateful boy who, luckily, grows up to see the error of his ways. This interpretation came in part from my father's liking to feel sorry for himself, to cast himself as the first to be overlooked and the last to know. In a rare good mood he played this role for laughs. But in a bad mood he took the slightest disagreement as a challenge to his experience and authority, and this left me, for years, feeling guilty that in disagreeing with him I had not given him the respect he deserved.

We rarely seemed to connect. One of the few times that we did was an instant, really, and it was so trivial that it is testimony to how ill at ease with each other we usually were. At a football game in the Yale Bowl, Father had on his homburg and a long, dark overcoat, every inch the gentleman. As we were walking to our seats, he farted. I heard it and giggled, looking up at him with amazed delight. "It slipped out," he said under his breath and winked.

We were alone often enough so that some deeper conversation might have been possible. It had the time to be coaxed

into life. I was five or six when my father began to take me on
house calls. At some houses he invited me in and gave me his
black bag to carry, the doc's little helper. Once we were inside
the family made a fuss over me. Yes, I did take after the only
good-looking one in the family, my mother, and yes, it would
not be long before I'd be big enough to eat the pasta off the
old man's head. Then he went into the sickroom, and I sat in
the living room, anxious not to be given anything to eat or
drink by these strangers. I breathed in the smells of illness and
answered their polite, boring questions about school. As often
as not I preferred staying in the car reading about Daniel
Boone or Thomas Jefferson in the Landmark biographies I
devoured or, if we had stopped for the mail, peering intently
at the bloody, wiggling slime of the lurid exposed organs and
horrible skin diseases on display in my father's medical jour-
nals.

We made rounds together at the hospitals ("horse pistols,"
my father joked), ate the fatty, pebble-skinned yellow chicken
breasts served for lunch in their cafeterias and, going home,
stopped at one or another of the drugstores my father did
business with. In these he roamed the aisles loading up on
toothpaste, shampoo, razor blades, soap, cigarettes for my
mother, a comic book or two for me and, if the store had a
liquor license, a bottle of scotch — all free of charge. Then
he paused to shoot the breeze. The talk was invariably of
gambling, football and baseball in season, but always the fights
and horses. When I began to follow college football, I was
dealt a stack of football betting cards that listed the week's
games and point spreads. My father always placed a buck or
two on the picks I made.

At first I clamored to go on house calls, but by the time I
reached twelve, the too-long waits in the car and the petting

in the houses and hospitals had begun to bore and embarrass me. It wasn't easy to say no to my father, and the excuses I manufactured were so lame that they provoked fights. "Go with your father," my mother urged. "Patsy, if the boy has something better to do and doesn't want to come with me . . ." "Go with your father. He doesn't get that much time to spend with you. Don't you want to be with him?"

"It's not that . . ."

"Patsy, don't force the boy. If he doesn't want to come there's enough for him to do around here. Let him mow the lawn, clean the garage or do something that's useful. I don't want to come home and hear he spent his time out playing with his friends or in his room reading."

Relief from these invitations did not come along until my brother, whose company my father preferred, was old enough to ride shotgun with him.

As a boy I had a goofy streak and did things that embarrassed my father, acts that I could not for the life of me explain. When I was old enough to know better, one such incident occurred. Workmen were putting in the swimming pool. Having changed out of my school clothes, I was in the bathroom naked when I heard them call for water. I didn't bother to dress but filled a pitcher, put glasses on a tray and brought them their drink. "September morn!" one of them cried out, and the others began to hoot and taunt me. When my father came home they greeted him with "What's the matter with that boy of yours, Doc? Doesn't he know how to dress himself yet?" and they told him that I had served them water naked. My incredulous father waved them off, angered by their crude humor at his expense and stung enough by their familiar tone to be humiliated. Over dinner that night, and for a few nights following, he asked again and again how I could do such a thing. Didn't I have any common sense? Tongue-tied by shame, I could not answer him. I simply did not know.

There were other similar interrogations over dinner. "Why did you do it? You must know why. No one does things without a reason. Look us in the eye and tell us why you did it. Why did you forge your father's signature on that detention card? And then brag about it! Why did you take one of those old guns of your father's from the attic to scare off those boys? What were they doing in the house running around in the first place? You ought to know better than that. How can we trust you to be alone? Do you need a baby-sitter at your age? Don't you care about what people in town think of your father? You know he's their doctor, and you ought to know by now that the kind of crazy, thoughtless things you do make him look bad."

This doctor's son theme ran through my childhood. I had to toe a straighter line, to mind my manners in public and to show respect unfailingly for my elders. I had to remember that the people in town I met were most likely my father's patients, and that they formed an impression of him through what I did. If I tried to buy cigarettes at a market, my father heard about it. If I tried to get comic books on credit at the drugstore, he'd be told. If I pulled the wig off that bald girl again, I could be sure my father would get another earful about it, and he did not want to talk with her angry parents a second time!

Did this have much of an impact on me? I liked to be noticed, to stand out in a crowd, but I did not care to be singled out as someone who ought to know better or set an example for others. I wanted attention on my own terms and not as a doctor's son. Perhaps an aspect of my contrary personality began to form here. My self-confidence obscures, if it does not hide altogether, a vulnerability that few ever see. I am gregarious but a loner, a man with many friends who keeps to himself.

My father had one thing in common with Claude Mench, he too was a street angel and house devil. In both of them I see myself. In my case, and perhaps in theirs as well, the devil is also an inner demon. When I am hard to live with, it is because I am finding it hard to live with myself, loath as I am to admit it at the times of my angry, demanding flare-ups.

What most infuriated my father about me were my "big ears" and bigger mouth. I inherited these faculties from my mother, or so he claimed, and he made no bones about wishing they had not been passed on. Adults were constantly warned that I was a "little pitcher with big ears." I prided myself on letting nothing get by me and still do. But then I took it for granted that everyone was interested in knowing just how quick and smart I was. My naturally secretive father resented me making his business mine and resented even more my broadcasting what I heard. This compromised his Old World sense of things, in which the father ruled and sons knew not to pay attention to what did not concern them, and to keep their months shut.

My father's decrees to speak only when spoken to never laid a glove on me. He found something womanish in my chatter, something loose, heedless and not to be trusted. My mother, on the other hand, encouraged her bright and talkative son. I knew by the age of twelve that I constantly spoke out of turn and said what was better left unsaid, but I could not control myself. To my father's chagrin and irritation, I did not get his message.

He sought to change my behavior by ignoring me or, when at the end of his rope, bluntly telling me, "Shut up!" The latter stung, but only enough to make me pause.

It has taken years for me to learn to hold my tongue, and to learn that I do not have to broadcast the fine degree of my powers of attention. Shame wore me down, but I had the good fortune to become a teacher, which has required almost more talk than even I had in me. Not that I am cured. I will forever be capable of saying out loud what should only be thought, and when I do I feel the remorse my father tried so hard to make me feel as a child.

By claiming these attributes for her side of the family, my mother encouraged my quick ears and gift of gab. In this as in my looks, my high forehead and long "German" nose, she saw a Mench, and this flattered me. Early on she let me feel that I was smart, and, at times, she hung on my every word. As a boy I had both her sense of fun and her naiveté about how others might respond to what I said. I was, as she had been, the class clown and once applauded . . . well, it was easy to mistake the whole world for an audience.

Our shared sense of humor often drove my father up the wall. There were times when we meant to do this. My motives may have been to create innocent fun, but I quickly fell into league with my mother and we ganged up on him. Understandably, he resented this and resented our use of him as an unwilling straight man. His stiff-necked attempt to rise above it egged us on all the more.

Secretly, I thought of myself as a Mench and fantasized happily returning with my mother to life in Pennsylvania. I knew these thoughts to be disloyal, and as much as they warmed me I accepted that they made me a criminal. This must have been part of their appeal. As with the thefts from

my father's pants pocket, I found being a Mench, being my
mother's fair-haired boy, irresistible.

I was eleven or twelve when my father became involved in his
first construction project. He went into partnership with Joe,
a carpenter several years his senior, who lived in a house he
had built for himself with his bawdy wife, Mary, and their
daughter, Claire. I do not know the details of how my father
and Joe became partners. I know more about red-faced, loud
Mary and the beautiful, black-haired Claire. They became
my mother's friends, and what I remember is a relationship
that grew tangled and then soured in step with my father's
dealings with the phlegmatic Joe.

   With the cash my father put up, the partners bought a few
acres of land off the main road in a neighboring town more
rural than our own. Their plan was simplicity itself — build a
modified Cape and sell it. Then invest some of the profits in
the next lot and repeat their success.

   The house went up slowly. Joe was a meticulous, taciturn
Swede, who had, as my father was to learn, a string of business failures and obligations that distracted him. My father
visited the site every few days, but my mother, at first, paid
little attention to the project. She did, however, befriend
Mary and was soon drawn in, willingly, to Mary's struggles
with the sullen Claire, who had just finished college. Later my
mother told me that Claire had declared herself a lesbian. According to my mother, Mary was both fascinated and re-
pulsed by this and determined to break up the affair Claire
was having with a college classmate. All her life my mother
had a weakness for the confidences of younger people. She
encouraged them, and soon Claire had begun to confide in

her and my mother had insinuated herself right into the middle of things.

As the house slowly neared completion, Joe required money to finish things off and to tide him over until the house sold and phase two of their plan went into effect. Irritated with his dawdling but impatient to get the house done and sold, my father grudgingly gave Joe the money and talked of getting a new partner.

The house did not sell but stood vacant through the fall and into the early winter. Joe, whose other troubles began to catch up with him, threatened my father with a suit unless he got his full share of the expected profits. He now claimed there had been no deal contingent on the sale of the house. My father quieted Joe with more money, but it caused Joe to press for the full amount he insisted was due him. At this point Mary came to my mother and told her that while she could use her help in dealing with my father she really did not need her putting her nose in Claire's affairs. Soon after, Claire, afraid she was about to lose my mother as her confidant, showed up in tears.

My parents, seeing themselves as having been taken advantage of at every turn, broke with Joe and Mary. The only option on the house was to rent it, and this my father did, but when the tenants proved irresponsible and had to be evicted, the house once again stood vacant. Joe continued his pestering, first by phone and then through a lawyer, but since he did not have a signed contract, my father said to hell with him. Finally, the house sold, and my father, blaming the small loss on Joe, wrote it off to experience. He had already become involved in a much more ambitious project, a housing development in Hamden, more than forty-five minutes east of Trumbull.

This time he went into business with several partners, one of whom, Julius Meshberg, my father came to characterize as the only Jew he knew who never made a dime. Julius and my father were to stay together, yoked like oxen, until the bitter end. Throughout their association Julius extolled my father as a doctor and a great man. When I went to work for what became the Tihamer Construction Company, Julius drove me to the houses we were building in Bethel and Danbury. As we drove he seemed to renew himself each morning by listing my father's virtues: loyalty, pride, intelligence, good judgment and integrity.

The Hamden development began with a great unrolling of street and sewer plans and architectural drawings of houses. The cigar-smoking partners met on Sundays in our family room, which Julius had remodeled out of my father's office. The other partners were as eager to throw thousands around in talk as my father was, but I cannot recall even one of them. I can see Julius arrive with the plans rolled under the arm of his belted suede jacket and hear him compliment my mother on her appearance. She cringed from him. She had disliked him from the start, and she never let my father forget this. I managed to stay to greet the partners and make myself a fly on the wall until, noticed, I was sent from the room.

The next thing I remember of Hamden is a stack of glossy eight-by-ten photographs. The partners are inspecting plans and gesturing across bare ground that has been chewed up by the bulldozers and dump trucks visible in the background. No future projects of my father's had such elaborate meetings, and none was documented by photographs.

Hamden died suddenly. Before a single foundation had been poured the plans fell apart. The town fathers, "thieves" I heard my father say over the phone, refused to issue permits for the sewers. The land had been prepared, roads started and schedules set under the assurance of the town's cooperation. But no sewers, no houses. There must have been more to it because, as Julius later said, the partners got pretty far into the deal. He lost his shirt, and my father lost a good chunk of money but earned Julius's respect by taking his lumps and not papering the others with lawsuits.

The Hamden deal may have come a cropper because a federal agency had been slow to consider an application for funds or had agreed to commit them and then reneged. There was angry talk of this over the phone. My father had left relations with the agency up to another of the partners, and they had been mismanaged. Despite this, my father continued to believe that you could borrow federal money and make it work for you, leaving the government with the risk and the shrewd businessman with the profits. In every one of his succeeding schemes he followed this course. Had he been in business during the savings and loans boondoggle, he might well have made himself the bundle he imagined.

After its demise, my parents worried about Hamden at the dinner table. My mother now complained that she had not liked the deal from the start. "What are you doing building houses? Didn't you learn your lesson with Joe? It's just pissing our money away. Bill, you don't know anything about building houses. You're a doctor and a good one, why isn't that enough for you?"

"Joe has nothing to do with this. Hamden didn't go bad because of anything I did. It was a good plan. I did it for you and the kids. What the hell else for? I do quite well, and you don't have a thing to complain about. You can't make money when a thief has his hands in your pocket. Next time that won't happen."

"Next time? With Julius? What are you doing with him? He gives me the creeps. He's the only Jew you'll ever meet who doesn't have a brain in his head, and your father has to do business with him. It's just pouring our money down a hole in the ground."

As soon as my mother enlisted us in her attack, my father clammed up. He hated to be challenged at his own dinner table. That fall several dinners ended with his slamming the kitchen door as he left for office hours and my mother clearing the table in tears. My father expected his wife and children to accept unconditionally his every word and deed. He indulged himself in the fantasy that his was an Old World family and he came home to be waited on hand and foot by adoring family members who sat down after he had finished dinner to gratefully eat the scraps of his meal. At times he played this role for laughs, and it was impossible to believe that he had ever taken himself seriously. Yet my father drew a line that we either refused to see or that was invisible to us. When we crossed it he did not hide his anger and hurt.

My mother had a taste for passionate and dramatic fights, real knock-down-drag-outs. She tenaciously pursued my father, and when she did, you could hear them fighting in their bedroom. For my mother these battles were cathartic. When they ended she forgot about them. Indeed, she forgot so quickly that it seemed there had been no principle at stake. My father, no less the self-dramatist, played out these battles, nursed them on an inner stage where he forever defended himself against those who would betray him. He cultivated the self-pity that draws pleasure from being misunderstood even as it curses, silently, those who misunderstand. My father found these enemies and endured his deepest betrayals at home.

Hamden quickly blew over, and my father, sobered by its failure, concentrated on medicine, where he made a very good living. Good enough so that there was money to send me to prep school, an investment in my future that a man of my father's standing could afford to make.

When the idea of going away to school, to "private school," first came home from the office, where my father had been talking about it with a patient, I could only shrug in response. I knew nothing of such places and neither did my parents, but they both knew it to be a step up, something they could do for me that their parents could not have done for them. They were also aware, as I was not, that the class they saw themselves entering sent their sons to prep school, and so men in uniform began to come to the house to interview me for military schools. My Nanny Mench grew lyrical about the Valley Forge cadets she had seen in their smart uniforms on Philadelphia's streets, and she offered to pay my way there. This offer, and the thought that my parents might accept it, caused me to squirm uncomfortably when interrogated by the gray-uniformed "colonels" who called at her house. I emphatically did not see myself in one of their uniforms.

We drove to Loomis, near the Massachusetts border, where the white-haired dean interviewing me suddenly asked if I could spell *believe*. "B-e-l-e . . ." Would I like to try again? Intimidated and feeling the heat from my embarrassed parents' eyes on the back of my neck, I stumbled again and wanted to sink beneath the cushions of the leather chair in which I sat. Next we toured Kent, but they wanted me to stay back a year and my father found this insulting. I had good grades, a big vocabulary from the reading I had done, and appeared to be quick and confident. I *was* quick, but hardly confident. In grade school I had been left to myself by teachers who had large classes and felt they had to concentrate on slower pupils. Besides I was the doctor's son, and it was assumed that I was smart. I knew my grammar to be shaky, and my mind went blank when I even looked at an algebra problem. An extra year at Kent might have been good for me, but the three of us had felt condescended to. We were definitely not for them.

We visited Wooster School last. Small, 110 boys and six buildings, one of which was a barn. The school had been recommended by a patient. On a smoky autumn afternoon, we were shown directly to the headmaster's office, where John Verdery greeted us. His ruddy handsomeness and appealing grin, the ease and welcome of his manner, won over my parents at once. He was thirty-eight that day, the same age as my mother, who, more than once, allowed as how John Verdery could "park his shoes under my bed anytime he wants to." A fantasy she had heretofore reserved exclusively for Cary Grant.

Wooster accepted me as I was, and that summer we bought my wardrobe at Brooks Brothers on Madison Avenue in New York City, and I read *The Catcher in the Rye* to prepare myself for what lay ahead. Late that September, weeks after my friends had started high school, my parents drove me the twenty-five miles to Danbury and school. The worlds of Trumbull and Wooster would prove to be so far apart that the distance between them might as well have been a thousand miles. I did not know it, but I had left home and would never be entirely comfortable there again.

A few years ago I taught for a time in a Boston prep school. I had not been in one since my years at Wooster. The faculty met four times a year for two days to discuss every one of the school's hundred and some students. As I participated in these meetings, I began to think of my own "career" (Wooster used this word while I was there) in school, and glimpsed the boy I had been as Wooster may have seen me.

When I write "the boy I had been" I claim no definitive understanding of him even now. Over the years he has been a bewildering number of boys to me. Time and distance have erased earlier certainties, and new insights have been replaced by others that had to be amended as I lived with my own children through their teens. Perhaps I do not know this boy any better now than I ever have, but sitting a few years ago at that table in the Commonwealth School library gave me a vantage point I had never had before. I saw that while I had been a mystery to myself, I had not been nearly so mysterious to Wooster's faculty. They had surely known other difficult boys like me.

At Wooster I was a painfully self-conscious extrovert. Self-conscious but not self-aware. My balance, uncertain as if I were on a teeter-totter, depended on how others regarded me. Yet I had no sense of how my actions might affect them. I took too much for granted, and this immaturity left me vulnerable. I wanted the world on my terms, but the world seldom cooperated, and its indifference left me hurt and confused. I had both my mother's brass and my father's capacity to be slighted, a combination that made for a heedless boy who often had wounds to nurse. Because I was stubborn and a slow learner, I had constantly to be taught the same lessons.

I remember what I wore the day I started at Wooster. When I had refused the Brooks Brothers clothes my mother picked out for me, we had our first of many tearful fights in that store. She won, as she would so many times, and that day I wore the "matching outfit" of brown pants, brown and green tweed jacket, light brown shirt and a brown and green striped tie. I felt as uncomfortable to be "dressed up" as I once had on the Fourth of July my mother had forced me to wear a pair of red pants in harmony with those worn by my brother and father.

We moved into my room, where my roommate had already claimed the bottom bunk. After a short faculty reception my parents, my mother dabbing the tears from her eyes, drove home. I went with my roommate to the school store, a room in the basement of the main building. I forget what supplies we bought, but I paid in cash and my roommate, Willie, wrote a check. As he carefully drew his name in large, round script, I said, "You have a nice hand."

"A what?"

"You have a nice hand, nice handwriting," and butter would not have melted in my mouth. Strange now to hear these words, their exact tone, echo in my mind. I knew then that the tone was one learned from my Pennsylvania grandmother, and I think I also knew that it was false — the tone of an insufferable little boy. Perhaps I remember it so clearly because it speaks to me of the false boy from which the real one, unpleasant as he certainly was, emerged.

"Don't you," my mother asked every time I called home, "feel homesick? Not even a little?" "No," I always replied, but this was not the exact truth. One absolutely clear and moonless night walking back to my dorm after dinner, I looked up at the very bright stars and my eyes filled with tears. I wanted to be back in the bowling alley where I had worked as a pinsetter, back in the smoke among the loud bowlers' voices, back setting pins quickly and smoothly, back listening to Elvis Presley's "Heartbreak Hotel" on the jukebox. I had no other homesick moments.

Through Thanksgiving I loved Wooster. I loved the freedom from home, the organized football, the unpredictable outbursts of wild laughter and my sense of a culture that I had to master and take my place in. I craved attention and got it when the Head, impressed by my glibness and the speed with which I had learned the outlines of the school's history, had me showing "prospects" and their parents around. I loved knowing what I knew of the school and loved, as well, being known. But as quick as I was on the uptake, I was slow in the classroom.

From the start I did poorly in algebra. My parents learned the word *block* to describe my difficulty, but I felt myself to be a dunce. I slogged through Latin showing the first signs of my failure with foreign languages. History and English were my best subjects, but in these I suffered, as I feared I would, from never having properly learned grammar. I talked a good game, but I was in over my head and knew it. Add to this my native streak of impatience — if things did not come easily my concentration began to unravel and soon my brains scattered. Restless, I got into trouble. Because I sincerely wanted to do well and be good, my behavior as "hacker" (our word for an idle, troublemaking wiseacre) and clown made me miserable.

At least I thought I wanted to be good. I knew I did not want to be in misery, to fail tests, to get caught reading Sherlock Holmes in study hall, to let my big mouth bring down on me the wrath of older, larger and stronger boys. But misery seemed the end result of every day. I went to bed swearing to myself that I would rise in the morning and do better, only to begin again as a chucklehead, all the more one because I believed that I had turned over a new leaf as I slept.

After Christmas I fell out with my roommate and moved into a single room. Glad to be by myself, I raised even more hell than before. It was usually me thumping hard on the floor or running down the hall that brought the master who lived on the floor below with his young family bounding up the stairs in a rage. One night before lights out he grabbed me by the throat. This young football coach was no friend of mine. He taught me algebra and browbeat me in class for my slowness. In return, I tormented him, and he paid me back, after which I complained to my parents about him. At first they took my side and together we began to take personally all my encounters with him.

A few days before spring vacation I came down with an extremely high fever. In its grip, or so it was later decided, I wrecked another boy's room, smashing his typewriter and tearing his clothes. If I did as I was accused I did not register it then and cannot remember having done it now. This act alone might have made me an outcast, but it did not. Instead, my high spirits and sharp and seemingly fearless tongue — I would say anything that came into my head — earned me friends, including, in time, the boy whose room I had been said to trash. I also earned my share of enemies.

But this account errs if it exaggerates my bolder self. Using the tones I learned from buttering up my grandmother Mench, I could suck up to Wooster's masters with the best of them. I was as frightened as anyone of bullies and a little scared of those older boys I wished to join but for whom I was little more than light entertainment. I did make friends with a senior who became my mentor in dressing Ivy League — tab-collar shirts, rep ties, khaki pants, white athletic socks, brown Weejun loafers, et cetera. When not occupied with his classmates he tolerated my admiration. I followed him into the shower and watched intently as with masterful strokes he shaved his freckled face.

By the end of that first year I had failed algebra and Latin, failures made abject by my solemn and totally unrealistic promises to my parents that I would pass both subjects. When the Head wrote them at the end of the year, he evaluated my performance as "too little too late." My mother, who had a taste for bromides of the Ben Franklin "Neither a borrower nor a lender be" sort, constantly repeated the Head's pronouncement throughout the rest of my academic career. The Head also ordered me to summer school, and thus I spent that summer taking the bus to Wooster, where five days a week I received private tutoring. I lightened the boredom of these bus rides by taking up smoking. Old Gold Straights, one after another until I made myself sick. I threw any number of half-finished packs from the bus window until, inevitably, the habit began to take.

In my second year, with being canned from Wooster a distinct possibility, I added smoking to my social vices. This meant sneaking into one of the school's several boiler rooms for a few drags, disappearing into the woods that surrounded the school or going into Danbury on Sundays for church services that I, and other smokers, "attended" in smoky corner spas. It thrilled me to flaunt authority, to fear getting caught and to enjoy the comradeship, the sign, of smoke. None of us smokers eluded the authorities for long. Some master or senior boy smelled smoke through the Sen-Sen on our breath, found cigarettes where we'd hidden them in our hollow metal bedposts or raided one of the boiler rooms just after we'd lit up. I was soon caught.

It seemed that I could not be a good Wooster boy so my unconscious determined that I would get the attention I sought by being a bad one. I quickly lost interest in my classes. Algebra and geometry I could not fathom, so what was the point of concentrating. Latin? I could have cared less. I read my Shakespeare, but I read with passion the paperback novels by Irving Shulman, *Rag Top* and *The Amboy Dukes,* that circulated in the school underground. In the late fall, on a night when I had the privilege of going into Danbury to a movie, I managed to get served a drink, a screwdriver, in a Danbury dive. I had just walked in and given my order. Knowing the status this discovery would confer upon me, I began to bring my friends there.

I did not stop at this unexceptional badness but began to show a streak of cruelty. That year I had a Jewish roommate, Andy Abrams, and my cruelty took the form of anti-Semitism. Abrams became a kike, mockie and Jewboy. Sorry, we're not serving matzo balls or gefilte fish for dinner even if for such a nice boy like you. I sang out these slurs until he attacked me. We fought until someone broke it up, and afterwards I treated him kindly for a time. Seeing that he had let his guard down, I went back to calling him a kike bastard. I have no idea why I went on like this. Abrams was my sole victim. I had no slurs for any of Wooster's other Jewish students. It is also inexplicable to me that Abrams, pummeling me with his fists and applying choke holds as he did, never reported my ugly behavior to the school authorities.

That New Year's Eve I swilled Cato's scotch from a fifth I had stolen from my parents' house. I drank so much so fast I blacked out and fell down two flights of stairs, where I lay filthy with blood, mud and vomit until friends carted me home in a wheelbarrow. The next morning my parents were hanging judges. My Nanny Mench had been home alone when the boys who dumped me on our front steps rang the bell and ran. She had thought I was dead, dragged me upstairs and cleaned me up, and *now* there was hell to pay. My grandfather called from Pennsylvania threatening to come up and smash every goddamned liquor bottle in the house. I sat staring at the breakfast I could not force myself to eat, throat on fire, head thundering, and endured the hammering of my parents' and my grandmother's sad, reproachful looks.

Back at Wooster, my grades scraping bottom, various mild penalties having been exhausted, I was placed on probation. This came without warning on a snowy day. During his after-lunch announcements, the Head summoned me to his office. At that very moment I looked out the dining room window to see my father's Cadillac pull into the school drive, and my stomach fell to my toes.

My father looked grim. I had a sullen smirk to meet that, but I had no defense against my mother. Her wide, wet eyes told me I had betrayed her completely. She carried a pair of winter boots for me, and these she threw to me as if to say, "We do this for you, everything for you, and this is the thanks we get in return!" In the Head's office, after listening to all that I had failed to do or had done wrong, my father, unexpectedly, began to argue. Not so much in my defense, but to challenge the Head's experience and knowledge. If Wooster really knew its business, my father insisted, such problems as I created would not exist. Somehow the school could not be doing its business. The Head reddened at this but fixed the blame on me in chapter and verse that silenced my father's bluster. He urged my parents to have me tested. Perhaps Wooster was not the place for me. Perhaps I could not do the work, could not be expected to follow the school's rules and ought to be somewhere more suited to my talents.

This session led to tense, tearful dinners when I came home for vacation and eventually to a series of meetings with an educational consultant in Bridgeport. I first went with my parents for an interview, the theme of which, set forth by my father, was that we are not convinced our son is as stupid as the school seems to think he is. (At twelve I had been a guinea pig for an experimental IQ test. This indicated, to my mother's enormous pride, my intelligence to be "near genius.") The consultant, a brown-suited, middle-aged man whose gold-rimmed spectacles gave him the look of a high school principal, advised several tests. I took these over the following days, alone at a desk in an otherwise empty room next to his office. I remember not a thing about them. In our next family interview we were told that the tests revealed my high aptitude for a career in either law or medicine. Upon hearing this my parents beamed.

Since I clearly showed such high aptitude while performing so poorly in class, it followed that I must be considered an "underachiever." My problem, the consultant adumbrated, was not intelligence but application. I had, the tests showed, poor study habits. I had to learn how to concentrate. Driving home, my parents agreed that they had learned a lot from the consultant. For both of them his words became the plow used to turn over and over my school failures, as yet another dinner got cold on my plate.

"We're not doing this for your own good," one of them began. "We're doing this because education is the one thing that no one can take away from you. We didn't raise you to be a ditchdigger, and thank God, Dr. Kern and his tests tell us you can be a lawyer or doctor if you want. But you have to apply yourself. The doctor made it clear that all the brains in the world and a dime will get you a cup of coffee. You are a *classic* underachiever. That's what John Verdery meant when he wrote 'too little too late.' You have to learn better study habits, and you do this by applying yourself. You do want to get into a good college, don't you? You're not going to let this all go to waste, are you?"

I ignored these words with perfect sullen indifference. Yet they remain vivid to me today. Much more vivid than the last sorry, wasted months of that school term. If my mother and father's "constructive criticism" failed to reach me, Jack Kerouac's prose did. That spring I read *On the Road* and knew upon finishing the book I must run away from Wooster. One dark, misty April night I waited for Abrams to fall asleep, packed a gym bag, walked down the back dirt road and passed the Danbury Fairgrounds before a car came by and, unbelievably, stopped to give me a ride. In two more rides I was fifteen miles from the school in Newtown, and there I stood in the rain without any idea where I was going. I had been to the Village in New York, and I guess I thought that was where I was headed, but I had no address in mind, no plan and, I soon admitted, not a prayer. I crossed the road and headed back to Wooster, shivering, in tears and hoping I could make it unnoticed. I did not want to increase my humiliation by getting caught.

I collapsed into bed just before the morning bell, and dragged myself to breakfast and through the days and through to the end of that term. Then I again rode the bus to Wooster and summer school. Dull days spent alone in a classroom with first my Latin and then my algebra teacher.

My parents continued to vent their concern by driving home the same points during dinner. I put on my mask of indifference, which served only to intensify their lecture. "It's not our fault that you've failed these courses and have to go to summer school. God knows it's not what we want for you. Is it, Bill? We would love to talk about something else and not give ourselves ulcers at dinner, but there is nothing more important to us than your future. It's important enough so that we're spending an arm and leg at summer school, but that doesn't seem to mean a damn thing to you. The point is that you're a smart boy, not as smart as you think you are, but smart enough to pass your courses or we wouldn't be doing this. If you don't like to hear what we're saying then you ought to do something to change our tune. But look at you, you sit there with a smirk on your face and nothing to say."

During my years at Wooster my father's yearly income reached its height. He expanded his practice, strengthened his connections with several convalescent homes, set aside his oft-proclaimed loathing for politicians long enough to arrange his appointment as coroner and medical examiner and kept his fingers out of other pies. He did take a flyer or two in the stock market with notable failure, but he had invested only peanuts. In 1958 he boasted that he took home over $75,000, and spent it as fast as he earned it. During these years my parents vacationed each winter in Bermuda or the Virgin Islands. They frequently drove into New York City for dinner and a show. New cars stood in our garage, new clothes filled our closets and none of this came on credit. Cash only. While my parents prudently reminded my brother and me that money did not grow on trees, they spent without a care.

My father grew expansive in other ways. During the early years of his practice, when he considered himself always on call, he did not take a drink. My mother sarcastically described him as "the life of the party." Their social life, she liked proudly to complain, had been all her doing. My father's success loosened him up and, although he had a low tolerance for booze, he began to enjoy a drink.

When he had his office remodeled into the family room, he had a bar built in, one that guests could belly up to, and here my parents began to entertain at what became larger and larger parties. In the summer they shifted their entertaining to poolside.

My father enjoyed serving his guests as bartender, pouring their poison — scotch, bourbon, Manhattans, Rob Roys, C.C. and water into wide highball glasses that were decorated with an image of a convict breaking rocks. Theirs was not so much a hard-drinking crowd as one that liked to get mildly looped in a hurry. These guests came dressed to the nines to flirt and joke. The parties quickly got raucous and "dirty" mouthed. Shortly after our marriage Beverly and I were asked to leave one so as not to intimidate the dirty joke telling.

Their humor ran to Rusty Warren ("Knockers up") and Belle Barth ("A trip around the world is not a cruise") party records, to joke shop signs picturing a sad-faced king under the motto "Every Ruler Doesn't Have 12 Inches," to cocktail stirrers shaped like African tribeswomen with large breasts pointing pertly up, to rubber nebbish dolls and smutty jokes on cocktail napkins. The barroom's most memorable joke stayed in a drawer until party time. It had been the gift of a friend. Around a fist-sized hole in a slab of pine board he had glued fur. All good laughs for those free and sophisticated enough to enjoy them.

The couples who came to these parties (there were no single men or women in my parents' set) had nearly identical backgrounds and aspirations. The doctors, lawyers and undertakers were, with one or two exceptions, the sons of immigrants. They had worked their way through state colleges, graduating at the end of the Great Depression, served in World War II and built practices that earned them comfortable livings. Some were better with money than others, a prime source of gossip, but all had their eyes fixed on the main chance.

They lived in bigger houses and wealthier towns than those they had grown up in. They honored their ethnic heritage by assuming that to be Italian, Armenian, Hungarian or Irish stamped indelibly their taste and character. They were mostly Catholic. In this my parents diverged as we observed no religion. They drove big cars, voted Republican, (at least until the advent of John F. Kennedy), got more exercised over the evil of socialized medicine than any other political issue, and counted on having successful children. They boasted of top grades and top colleges. Through my first two years in prep school my failures were so embarrassing to my parents that they had to be hidden. When they listened politely to the success stories of Carol Esposito or Bunny Romano it hurt, my mother reminded me, because I had let them down, had let myself down, so badly.

The wives of these professional men were, every one of them, homemakers. They had often heard their husbands proclaim, "No wife of mine will ever work!" Like their husbands these wives expected to pile up a fortune, and they looked forward to lavishing this on their children and their friends. The few who did not share this desire by displaying wealth and hospitality were condemned for their niggardliness. All of them agreed with my parents that money did not grow on trees, but they acted as if they had entered a forest, a preserve especially created for them. Throughout the late fifties, as I became increasingly aware of my parents' world and values, and worked to separate myself from both, they and their friends were on the same upward curve.

I should say that I *labored* to separate from my parents. It was not easy, and I was not forthright about it. I hid from them all that I could and lied to them about what I was sloppy in hiding. In my case this hiding and lying had the opposite of its desired effect. I again saw myself as a criminal and un-worthy of my freedom. Guilt over failing my parents hobbled my efforts to separate. And as my parents insinuated them-selves more deeply into my life through their friendship with the Verderys and Braiders at Wooster, I became bound still closer to them.

My parents and their friends lived in a small, totally white (except for maids), middle-class world. They accepted with-out question America's greatness in all things, and believed that if you could not get what your heart desired in the US of A then you must be inferior in body or soul. They ac-cepted the status quo that benefited them, and in their inno-cence believed this to be the true way of the world.

Between my sophomore and junior years I got religion, aca-demically speaking. Where I had been flunking courses I now made the honor roll. Where I had never been out of com-pulsory evening study hall, I was now free to study in my room. Where I had been on probation with one foot out of the school, I was now a nearly exemplary boy. What hap-pened? I have no idea. Sudden maturity? Improbable. Fed up with the misery brought on by failure and the gut-twisting dinners at home? Yes, but I had worn out a dozen pledges to do better. A newfound intellectual interest? Not at the start of the year but later, and this came as a direct result of my French teacher, Donald Braider, and his family.

The Braiders actually came to Wooster my sophomore year, but I had only casual contact with them then. Except for their youngest child, Jackson, a wonderfully skinny, elastic kid with a rubbery mug of a face. He was four or five and a plea-sure to play with, squeeze, rub his short-haired skull and toss in the air because he so loved the roughhousing. Jackson became something of a mascot to a few of the boys, and I particularly liked him and he liked me. But I had not a thought of Jackson or the Braiders during the summer I spent riding the bus to Danbury and the tedium of summer school.

A few weeks into the fall, this was 1958, Donald Braider asked me to baby-sit. The only writer on the faculty, he had just published his first novel, *The Palace Guard*. I had not read the novel nor had I been inside his house before. He wanted me Saturday night for dinner.

Donald, Carol and their children, Christopher, Susan and Jackson, lived in a large farmhouse owned by the school on a dirt road not more than a half mile off campus. I arrived just as ginger-haired Carol, smoking a cigarette and drinking a glass of wine, served spaghetti to the children, to me and to Bucky, their standard French poodle, who sucked his meal from a plate set on the table! Donald poured himself wine from a gallon jug and filled a glass for me. My family did not drink before or with meals, though their subsequent friendship with the Braiders would start them doing so, and I had never had more than a sip or two of wine, a drink thought in my home to be foreign and bohemian. I tried to accept the glass as nonchalantly as Donald offered it. I certainly wanted that glass of wine, indeed, from the moment I sat at their table, I wanted the entire Braider family, wanted to be their number-one baby-sitter and wanted, as I would with other families on whom I developed crushes, to wipe out whatever separated them from me. That the Braiders, all of them, indulged me and never made me feel like the pest I must sometimes have been, is a graciousness I love them for to this day.

I ate that first raucous dinner whose mess and dirt had glamour for me. My mother, like her mother before her, prided herself on keeping a spotless kitchen, in which you cooked, you ate and then you cleaned up so thoroughly that all evidence a meal had taken place disappeared. In Carol's kitchen there was dog hair, kids' toys, empty wine jugs, overflowing ashtrays and the sort of litter my grandmother cursed as dreck. Grease and crusty residue speckled Carol's stove. A big red and yellow box of kosher salt sat atop it, and to the side stood heavily fingerprinted bottles of olive oil, vinegar, soy sauce and others whose labels I could not read. The kitchens I knew had Formica surfaces that shone, and refrigerators that could have just stepped out of magazine advertisements. Carol's fridge held food in pots and on platters and plates, uncovered food with its sauce congealed. Such naked food never went into our family refrigerator. It disgusted my parents. As a boy I had been put off by the smells in my friends' kitchens and made excuses about just having eaten to avoid taking meals in them. Given this, my instant attraction to the chaos of Carol's kitchen and its rich mix of smells remains as mysterious to me as the 180-degree turn my academic work took that year.

I knew at once what drew me to the rest of the house — books. There were books everywhere. Books stacked on tables, some with pipe cleaners for place marks, books on windowsills, on coffee tables, hall tables, on the bathroom floor and in shelves, overflowing them in every room. As a reader who had grown up in a virtually bookless house (my room held the only bookshelves, which my father had a carpenter build to get the books off my floor), I felt, although I could not have put it this way then, that entering the Braiders' I had come home. Every house I have lived in since has been filled with books. Carol Braider saw at once the effect the books in her house had on me. In the library at the front of the house, which doubled as Donald's study, she came upon me one day looking once again through the slim volumes of poetry. "You'll have books like this one day," she said as if stating a foregone conclusion.

In dreams I often return to the rooms of my childhood home to take part in or observe some action that I have moved there from my present life. This is unremarkable and so would it be if the Braiders' house provided a similar dreamscape, but it does not. Instead, when I am browsing in a secondhand bookstore, head tilted, slowly going along the rows of titles, a book will jolt me back to the Braiders'. It is usually a Grove Press book with the recognizable logo, a downward pointing arrow, on its spine. Donald had roomed in college with Barney Rosset, Grove's publisher, and since Rosset sent the Braiders every new Grove title, the house was full of them. I frequently buy the Grove titles I come across, even those I do not intend to read, because they return me to the Braiders' living room.

And there were abstract paintings on the walls, the likes of which I had only previously seen in a *Life* magazine and fervently responded to without in the least knowing why. These pictures, net- or nestlike swirls, were by Jackson Pollock, a friend of the Braiders when they ran a Long Island bookshop and their son's namesake. There were dark pictures, black and brown saillike forms, by Pollock's wife, Lee Krasner. Out of an oval frame sprouted a junk shop with a cue ball and spikes at its center by Alphonso Ossorio. There was a Picasso head of a boy, white on a dark ground, bought in Paris, a few bold black girders by Franz Kline on pages ripped from a telephone book, and upstairs, in the guest room where I spent several nights, a Mary Cassatt landscape. I had to be told who she was, who they all were, and I was eager to know what I could about them.

Two living room "sofas" were French cribs with iron bars for sides and backs and hard, flat cushions. Exotic and uncomfortable. All the easy chairs were worn, their upholstery stained, and of a comfort that invited you to throw your leg over their arm. All the tables, wooden chairs, lamps and rugs had been lived with and were not the showpieces that filled my own home. I found it all touched with glamour. I also found Carol's raincoat splattered with red house paint glamorous. Returning home after the bohemian freedom of the Braiders' house, I felt more than ever that the rooms I had grown up in were lifeless.

In the Braiders' living room stood a large armoire that held their hi-fi system and their huge, to my eyes, record collection. Besides my parents' off-color party records that were kept in plain brown sleeves in a closet, I had the only real records in our house, rock 'n' roll singles and the few jazz LP's that marked a recent interest. It was at the Braiders' I first heard (and was told I could play while baby-sitting) Charlie Christian, Serge Chaloff, Norman Granz's JATP concerts, Count Basie. And Bix Beiderbecke, one of the foundations of my love for jazz.

I knew at first sight that these books, pictures and records, that the house's free-spirited clutter and comfort, were for me. Nothing in my upbringing had prepared me for the Braiders. As with the voice that first spoke a poem in my mind, the Braiders' house and their way of living chose me. But the physical facts of their life were only part of the education I got from the Braiders.

Both Donald and Carol gave me the gift of their attention. At home my father had little time for the question boy and motor mouth that I was. My mother encouraged me, partly, I think, to irritate my father. He had only contempt for her hanging on my every word and loathed the way she asked me questions over dinner to get my opinions of their friends. If my father saw me as pretentious, my mother liked to deflate my cockiness by provoking arguments. I was easy to get a rise out of and leapt into these arguments only to be frustrated by her shifting the subject or pulling rank on me.

Not only did the Braiders open their home and library to me, but they had time for my sixteen-year-old run-on stream of discoveries, questions, puns, jokes, school gossip, opinions and snap judgments. Certainly, they humored me at times, but I felt their interest in me to be genuine. Perhaps they instinctively knew that I was a boy who needed to talk to know what he thought, needed to hear himself think out loud. If I especially remember Donald's attentions in this regard, it is because I came to him more often with questions about books, writers and writing. He had an ample store of knowledge and anecdotes about all three. I did not know it then, but he taught me that one value of literature is pleasure.

Because I wanted to engage Donald's attention as completely as I could and on his own terms, I plunged into books that were a little over my head, into William Styron's (a Braider friend) *Set This House on Fire,* Norman Mailer's *Advertisements for Myself,* two thick books bound in paper the color of shirt cardboard on the Hollywood blacklist, Iris Murdoch's *The Bell,* (an enthusiasm of Donald's I could not share), A. J. Liebling, Joyce Cary, Trollope, Italo Svevo . . . To paraphrase Oscar Wilde, I pursued the luxuries while letting the necessities take care of themselves. Once again, my father's warnings notwithstanding, I ran before I could walk. But this time I did so with someone to coach and correct me, someone who encouraged me to follow the lead of one writer to another, to go from Styron to James Baldwin and

Jack Kerouac, (whom I thought of as my own discovery), and to Ezra Pound, whose Chinese poems thrilled me into declaring to myself that I must be a poet.

Three events then occurred to give shape to this ambition. That winter Donald Braider and another teacher, Donald Schwartz, in whose doghouse I stood as firmly as I did in Braider's favor, got together a discussion group of juniors and seniors interested in writing. For the first meeting we read T. S. Eliot's "The Love Song of J. Alfred Prufrock." A visiting Neil Rudenstine, Phi Beta Kappa graduate of Princeton, Rhodes Scholar and Wooster's brightest star, guided us through the poem. Neil, for all his triumphs a most unassuming young man, skillfully pointed out what Eliot was up to, with asides from Braider and Schwartz, while keeping our ears on the poem's shifting tones.

Awed by the level and precision of Rudenstine's attention, I thought to myself that if this was poetry with a capital *P* then the few poems I had written were scribbles, nothings. What I heard in "Prufrock" came from another place, loftier and beyond any literary world I had previously been exposed to. Somehow, I knew that this world was not for me. Too arid and intellectual. I felt I could not belong to it and thus did not want to. Here, as with much of my academic success of that year, I thought myself a fraud. How could I pass myself off as a poet, even as someone interested in poetry, if I could not accept and aspire to the standard set before me? I did not know how to say this to Donald Braider or to anyone else.

That spring, at a school party, my mother came across the grass through a crowd of teachers, parents and my fellow students waving a newspaper and calling excitedly, "Have I got a surprise for you!" My father must have been at her side, but I can see only my mother's green suit, her wide grin, the flapping paper and the faces turned toward me. I didn't know what to think.

Her surprise was the *Trumbull Times,* our hometown weekly paper. As a few people crowded around, she opened it to a page of my poems, my name in caps and, gasp, a photograph of me captioned, "Bill's mother says he looks more like a football player than a poet." I froze in embarrassment. Everything stopped. In my numbed state I could not even think of waking up from this nightmare. I had the paper in my hands and was reading the caption when I knew all I wanted was to disappear, to die.

When I did focus I saw that the poems were those I had written during the previous year and hidden under old clothes in my bureau at home. I had not known that my mother routinely snooped through my room, looking for whatever incriminating things a boy's mother looks for. Finding the poems, she took them, without asking me or getting my father's advice, to the editor of the *Times,* Jerome Boin, who printed them without so much as a by your leave to me.

My mother's skills as a stage mother aside, Boin may have been moved to do what he did because of my father's standing in town. I am sure he would have been less likely to publish the poems of the town plumber's son, but then that poet's mother might not have forced them upon him. (I later worked under Boin and found him to be a humorless straight arrow.) How my mother cajoled Boin into publishing the poems without my permission I do not know. I could not bear to discuss the matter with him, and as for her, I had all I could do to try to convince her that I hated seeing my poems in the paper.

"Oh, no you don't," she said, waving me aside. "You love

it and I know you do. Your name in print! A big deal all over town and at Wooster! I know you, you love it."

To this day I rarely send out poems to magazines. Fear of rejection plays its part in this, but I can trace much of my reluctance to what my mother and her accomplice Boin did.

I had a delayed reaction to the third event. On a sunny Saturday morning the Braiders sat with houseguests having breakfast on their front porch. Because I had baby-sat and slept over I too was there. The guests were the painter Mike Goldberg and his wife, the writer Patsy Southgate. As the four adults talked, Goldberg and Southgate told the Braiders about a poet named Frank O'Hara, who, they laughed, kept his pot in a coffee can buried in someone's backyard. I had never heard O'Hara's name before and had no idea any of this had stuck in my memory until two years later, when I encountered his name, and those of Patsy and Mike, in Donald Allen's anthology *The New American Poetry*. Because I "knew" these people, I felt an immediate connection with O'Hara's poems. Remembering his name as I did has always seemed an omen to me.

A few weeks after my mother waved the newspaper for all to see, the Braiders invited my parents to their house for dinner. Since I had done nothing but talk about the Braiders, my parents were eager to go. The dinner lasted until dawn. Back at home, giddy with the excitement of it, my mother phoned me with details of the meal, thrilled to have talked the candle down about me and the school. Opposites had found each other attractive. She passed on Donald and Carol's words of praise, and I was flattered to hear them. I very much wanted the Braiders to like me, and they did. This pleased me, but I was even more pleased that my parents had made such a hit

with the Braiders. This confirmed a level of acceptance unknown, I thought, to other Wooster boys.

The summer before my Wooster senior year, I worked as a
soda jerk, read John O'Hara, took the train in to New York's
Five Spot to hear Ornette Coleman, drove my mother's sky
blue Buick Roadmaster convertible out on dates with my
first serious girlfriend and began to think about college. Began, that is, to visit colleges and worry that I might not be accepted by an Ivy League school. Like all good Wooster boys,
I dreamt of the Ivy League, and this too is what my parents
had their hearts set on. I visited Brown with my mother, and,
on the way to Jim Thorpe, stopped at Lafayette in Easton,
Pennsylvania, by myself. Lafayette accepted me in the interview. I saw their panting interest as pathetic and ruled out going there. I set my sights on Brown, whose response to me
had been lukewarm.

When we discussed colleges over dinner, my parents began
by saying that while I could go anywhere I really wanted to I
ought to understand that a C at Harvard or Brown meant two
or three steps on everyone else, open doors and money in the
bank. Not that I had to go to Harvard, although that wasn't
out of the question, but that any Ivy League school guaran-
teed more than just an education. "You'll meet people there,
make friends and contacts," my father assured me, "that will
stay with you and help you for the rest of your life."

I could dismiss these clichés, but inwardly I felt the
pressure of my parents' expectations, and the pressure of
Wooster's as well. Like most of my classmates, I had learned
to believe that the college I got into would be a fair measure
of my worth as a person, intellectually and otherwise. This
article of faith went unpublished at Wooster, and when

enunciated it was denied, but even the most innocent third former knew it to be the truth. He knew the words to mock the acceptee to Bates, Defiance or Rollins, and he would use them.

Still, discussing college over dinner with my parents, rather than having another postmortem on my academic shortcomings, was a blessing. It opened up new areas of contact with my parents, as did my romance with my girlfriend, Mary. She was the first girl I brought to the house, and my mother leapt to enlist her as an ally. She gossiped about me, even in my presence, pretending that for all my orneriness I was really an open book to both of them. They could, my mother winked to Mary, see right through me, and Mary, whose own mother was strait-laced and cold, ate this up.

My parents soon urged Mary and me to join them for dinners out and trips to New York. Eager to feel more sophisticated than our peers, we accepted. A mistake. These invitations were soon thrown in my face. Whenever I had done something that my mother could label "ingratitude," she read me her litany. "We've given you a swimming pool, a prep school education, a beautiful house, and we take you and your girlfriend with us everywhere. Name me other parents that generous. And what do we get in return?"

My mother's Buick frequently made this list. Since we lived in the suburbs, and I did not have a car of my own, I depended on my mother's generosity with her snazzy convertible. To get the use of the car I had to mow the lawn, clean my room and endure lectures on how I should be doing more around the house. Nothing exceptional in that, but my mother had other hoops to put me through.

Her eagle eye had noted the first blemish to appear on my face, and every pimple and blackhead that followed brought a war whoop from her. "Oh, that's a real headlight you have there, a volcano, a regular Vesuvius! You could get a job in a bakery filling éclairs!" Then she picked up Wooster's slang, zits and bogots. I fought her off, but she was relentless. She wanted a "pick," and she offered money and kept after me until I gave in. Or she used her car as the carrot, and I gave in more quickly. And so in return for squeezing the pus from the pimples and blackheads on my face, an operation that began with a hot washcloth to draw the stuff to the surface and ended with an astringent to sooth bruised pores, I could drive Mary out on our next date.

My senior year I did as well academically as I had the year before but, despite the hot breath of college, no better. My friendship with the Braiders held firm. Carol came down sick that winter, and I lived in the house for days at a time looking after the kids while she kept to her bed. In the spring the Verderys asked me to live at their home and baby-sit their three boys while they were traveling in California. This meant I could drive their tiny Morris Minor back and forth to Danbury to fetch their son Ben, Jackson Braider's soul mate, from school. This completed my transformation from problem boy, but new status as trusted baby-sitter did not curb my wayward tongue. One lunch at the Head's table he started a sentence, "I've been thinking . . . ," and not missing a beat I finished it, "and we can smell the wood burning." The other students gasped. He shot me a hard look. I toughed it out but felt miserable because there seemed some imp inside me that I was powerless to control.

When college letters arrived in April, my improved academic and social standing meant nothing. Thin envelopes meant rejection; fat ones, you were in. When Brown's thin envelope came, I called my mother in tears, desolate over having failed my parents, Wooster and myself. I heard a similar desolation in her voice. She had no words to make the prospect of Lafayette, a backwater unheard of at Wooster, bearable.

On graduation day, when many of my classmates cried, I did not. I had strong feelings about Wooster, but tears could not express them. Except for failing to achieve an Ivy League college, I took away from Wooster much that my parents hoped I would. To my mother's delight I now stood when ladies entered the room, yes-ma'amed, no-ma'amed and sirred, called my father "Father," was quick to please and thank you and had, in her mind, passed through the rebellious phase that had so bewildered her. As usual she passed on to me my father's praise for my accomplishments, such as they were, and told me how proud he was of me. He certainly took pride in his new friendship with the Braiders and Verderys, and perhaps he felt I had been partially responsible for this. He proved to be a generous friend, using his connections to supply them with cases of wine at wholesale prices, and, when the Verderys spent a year in France, my father sent regular shipments of prescription drugs and the Head's favorite pipe tobacco.

For my part I had Donald and Carol's encouragement. I may have written no more than a dozen poems and had acres of books to read, but they took seriously my interest in books and writing. I also left Wooster with a developing social consciousness. This came directly from the handful of black students at the school and Wooster's intense pride in them. Similar schools had no black students, and Wooster was aware, to the point of smugness, of how its black students set the school apart. In my case it was their presence and not their persons — I disliked most of them and was cruel to some —

that influenced me. In combination with rock 'n' roll music, James Baldwin's essays, Ralph Ellison's *Invisible Man* and my parents' garden-variety prejudice, Wooster's attitude rubbed off on me, and my views on race began to take shape, views that soon drove a wedge between me and my parents.

Growing up in Trumbull, the only black people I encountered were Sam Farrar, who emptied the town's septic tanks for a living, and the cleaning ladies who came to our house. Once a week they rode out by bus from Bridgeport's housing projects. When I was little Big Mary let me ride horsey on her broad back as she scrubbed the kitchen floor. One day, my mother being out, Mary made me lunch. I was not more than eight. She cooked and served me a grilled cheese sandwich, but because it came from her brown hand I could not force myself to eat it. She surely knew what was in my mind when I wrapped the sandwich in a napkin and explained that I meant to save it for later. I carried it up to my room, where I hid it at the bottom of my toy box.

I remember we once drove Mary home to the barrackslike brick project where she lived. As we rode away my father shook his head and pointed at the junked cars and garbage in the parking lot near Mary's door. "They make shit out of everything," he declared. By the time I first tuned in Alan Freed's rock 'n' roll show, I had long been exposed to the racist virus inherent in America's white suburbs.

I had been introduced to rock 'n' roll by a friend's older sister. When Elvis Presley emerged I already knew the music, and his appearance on the Tommy Dorsey television show thrilled; my first love was rhythm and blues, black music. Night after night, as I did my homework before our console radio, I listened to Freed's WINS show hearing the Moonglows, LaVern Baker, Ray Charles, the Penguins, Ruth Brown and Clyde McPhatter and the Drifters.

One night, as he readied himself to go to the office for office hours, my father paused to listen. "That's nothing but nigger music. You can't really be enjoying that noise."

"It's good . . . I like it . . . what . . ." I knew I had been attacked, and scrambled to defend myself.

"Well, it's nigger music, jungle music. You'll get over it."

"I don't want to get over it. I like it. You don't know."

"No, it's you who doesn't know. I heard this when I was your age. Music just like it. Nigger music. And that's all your Elvis the Pelvis plays. Nigger music. Someday you'll understand that your father knows a thing or two." He laughed a harsh laugh at my innocence.

I burned inside. I took my father's contempt for the music personally. These black voices touched me in a way baseball, biographies or my interest in archaeology never had. What was I supposed to get over? I knew my father was wrong, wrong about the music and wrong about me. Gradually, I came to understand how wrong I thought he was.

When I entered Wooster, the seniors listened to Lester Lanin's "'S Wonderful," and that spring they mooned over Johnny Mathis crooning. We younger boys were not allowed radios or record players, but I kept my ears peeled for rock 'n' roll, and soon, through an older boy in the school's music room, I discovered jazz. This coincided with access to the Braiders' records and my first reading of James Baldwin's essays. I began them in total ignorance of the Harlem Baldwin describes. Knowing nothing of that world but what he told me, I knew, because of my father's attitude, that Baldwin's fury was justified.

I discussed Baldwin's essays with the Braiders, and in the classroom we several times discussed race, especially when studying *Huckleberry Finn*. When I brought up the subject at home, my parents rolled right over me. I did not know what I was talking about, could not know since I had no experience and had not seen what my mother and father had seen. I got everything I thought from a book. Until I saw with my own eyes I had better not let my mouth run away with me.

When I read Ellison I kept my mouth shut. Soon I never brought up the subject of race at all. I played my jazz records when my parents were out of the house. But, of course, race proved impossible to avoid, and so I had to listen to more than one variation of their filibuster. I would grow out of the nonsense that books had put into my head. I was an idealist who would have to learn the hard way. They held to this line through the rise of Martin Luther King and during the opening months of the Vietnam War. My father and I argued about that too, but he vanished before we got very far.

Wooster left its mark in other ways, too. Donald Schwartz habitually picked up litter off the school grounds. This met with catcalls from most of us. Now, walking a Vermont back road, I catch myself picking up a beer can and see my reflex going back to Wooster. I also learned from Schwartz that the way the New Critics read could not satisfy me. In teaching their approach, he ruled out the world as we students experienced it. I wanted to be right in the ways that Schwartz demanded, but I could not accept that poems exist on a plane above and outside the world I lived in. If poems have nothing to do with the time in which they were written and nothing to do with who wrote them, then what of the poems I was writing? They came from my world and my response to words and not from some desire for perfection or to commit irony. Could they be without value?

In the spring of my senior year, returning from a school baseball game in upstate New York, we crossed the Hudson River where the World War II cargo ships filled with surplus grain were moored. Back at Wooster, I immediately wrote a poem about this ghost fleet. How could this poem, this impulse, rise above its moment and attain the well-wrought perfection demanded by the New Critics? Wouldn't the reader want to know, have to know, something about World War II and surplus grain? Was poetry to avoid the facts of our lives? If the New Critics were right, then my poems could never measure up. This thought troubled me longer than it should have.

At Wooster I first encountered the smugness peculiar to private American academic institutions. I have seen it since on Harvard's public face and in its private heart. And at Brown and Wellesley, where I have also taught. In school after school this smugness has a life of its own. It gives such comfort that those who teach and administer cannot see that it exists or, for the most part, hear how it sounds. They depend that much upon it.

It seemed that the good things Wooster stood for, its championing of black students, its genuine care for difficult boys like me and its blurring of the lines between students and teachers, children and adults, could not be accepted for what they were. They had to be promoted as superior to how other schools conducted their business. Perhaps it was my distaste for this smugness, and my inability to grant Wooster special status, that kept me from crying at graduation. But more likely it was the contrariness that has led me so often to do the opposite of what is expected of me.

I also left Wooster with a sharp and cutting tongue, a "rapier wit," or so I fancied. I had learned to tease at my grandfather's knee, and I came to Wooster prepared to indulge this habit. Through my two miserable years I could be merciless to those boys who were the school victims, and, because I led with my tongue, to nearly everyone else if the opportunity arose. I cruelly hurt boys who could not take it, and laughed at the pain I inflicted. This "wit" was an aspect of my personality that tended to amuse my mother. My father thought it extremely unpleasant. "I do not find that sort of thing funny" was what he said, and for once he did not elaborate.

As a farewell gift Wooster gave each of us graduates a leather-bound copy of *The Oxford Book of Christian Verse*. John Verdery inscribed mine, "It has been good for Wooster to have you around." I thought he was being kind, and when I followed his "see page 119" I knew it. On that page appears Robert Herrick's poem "His prayer for Absolution." It asks God to blot out his "unbaptized rhymes,/ writ in my wild unhallowed times."

For my graduation my parents gave me a brown and cream secondhand 1950 Pontiac sedan, and I drove home with Peter, who would enroll in Wooster in two years. I worked that summer filling orders in a drug wholesale house. My romance with Mary continued through so many frustrating petting sessions that by fall we had tortured each other into a breakup. As I packed to leave for Lafayette, my father, unbeknownst to the family, set about launching the successor to the Hamden debacle, the Tihamer Construction Company.

When I began Wooster my father ordered me to write my mother. Every Wednesday lunch we were required to turn in a letter home or be dismissed from the dining hall. Several times, having no letter, I stuffed a napkin into an addressed envelope, and once, to my mother's great amusement, I wrote, "Dear Mother — It's Wednesday and so I thought I'd drop you a line" and drew a line down the page to my signature.

My father gave me the same order the day he, my mother and brother moved me into my Lafayette dorm. "It doesn't matter," he told me, "if you write me, but you have to write your mother and you have to do a better job of it than you did at Wooster. Your arm won't fall off in the effort. And I expect you to get your hair cut when you come home!" He gave me a twenty-dollar bill, shook my hand and they drove away.

I had little use for Lafayette when I started, and I graduated with the same bad attitude. In the thirty years since graduation I have returned twice, and I see but one friend I made there. At Wooster we had been warned that freshman year in college might be relatively easy after the workload we were used to. Mine proved to be easy enough that I did almost no work outside my English composition class. There, Donald Haberman introduced me to Isaac Babel, whose stories I continue to read every year, to Chekhov's great story "Gooseberries," to Thornton Wilder's *Our Town,* which Haberman taught as a satire, and to *A Casebook on Ezra Pound,* which furthered and deepened my lifelong interest in this poet. It was Haberman who gave me the only advice I carried away from Lafayette: "Be true to your vulgarities." He said it in response to my too quick disowning of something, Presley's music perhaps, that I really did like but could not admit because I knew it to be in bad taste. It took me years to gain the confidence to follow Haberman's words and stand up for the peculiarities of my own taste regardless of what others thought.

Haberman also spoke sharply to me in conference after I had complained about my parents. I must have been whining about their not understanding me. I'm sure I was fishing for sympathy, and that I hoped by confiding in Haberman to ingratiate myself with him. But what I said was harsh enough to provoke the man. "That's no way to talk about your parents," he snapped at me. "It is difficult to trust someone" — he looked me right in the eye, a look I shifted away from — "who talks about his parents with the lack of respect you've just shown. You know you really do not mean what you just said."

Stung, I thought about his words as I walked across campus. I know I felt that I had blundered in attempting to win him over by bad-mouthing my parents, by assuming that a flippant tone about them somehow made Haberman and me equals. I wanted his attention but had asked for his sympathy. It was this that he wouldn't give me, this that caused him, I thought, to say I didn't mean what I said. Now I see that I had a premonition that my parents and I were spinning apart, and the only way I could put this was to exaggerate the distance between us. I also see that I wanted another admired adult to take my side, as I thought the Braiders had, and help me separate from my parents.

Tall, sweet natured, droll and sad faced, Haberman tried to befriend me. He asked me to baby-sit for his infant daughter, and when he and his wife came home he offered me a beer so that we could have a moment to talk. He pressed on me William Gaddis's *The Recognitions,* which I struggled through with profit. In response to his asking me what recent book I had enjoyed the most I gave him *The Rack* by A. E. Ellis. I'd bought the book because of a high-toned *New York Times* review but found it so dull I had not been able to finish it. Because I did not know yet how to be true to my vulgarities, I did not give him William Burroughs's *Junkie* or the Kerouac novel I was reading. I may have thought that Haberman was just being polite and would never actually read *The Rack*. But he did and asked me, incredulously, how I'd managed to drag myself through it. I mumbled a response, but, again, he had caught me out.

From my friendship with the Braiders I had developed a veneer of sophistication. I earnestly did want to read all the books I claimed to have read and see all the movies I said I had seen, but I knew I was too much the phony to hold up my end of an intellectual friendship with Haberman. I avoided him so he would not see through me. One day he stopped me to ask if there was something the matter, some reason why I no longer stopped by his office to chat. I backed away with a lame excuse and began to dodge him more cleverly. Today I still dream of the man, dreams in which we meet by chance and after I tell him the truth we fall into the deep soul talk we never had at Lafayette.

In the dormitory my behavior marked me as eccentric. I placed my mattress on the floor, and I listened to folk music, to Odetta, Reverend Blind Gary Davis and Robert Pete Williams, all cat screech and mumbles to my basketball star roommate from East Orange, New Jersey. He retired at ten each night, sleeping under a black mask while I stayed up late smoking Camels and working on a novel, "In the Crystal Palace" (a phrase from Dostoyevsky's "Grand Inquisitor"), whose opening twenty pages I wrote and rewrote over the next four years and could never get beyond.

I fell in love at a mixer, a romance that went bumpily along until it ended for me weeks after it had for her. Over midyear break, my 1950 Pontiac threw a rod outside Albany, New York. I was on the way to see dormmates and neglected to check the oil. I arrived behind a tow truck. This was the first of several cars that I, in Louis Kaye's phrase, "made shit of." At the time my father threatened all manner of punishment, but he cleaned up after me, seeing to it that the Pontiac got disposed of. Then he bought me another car, a finned Plymouth convertible. I wrecked this one too. My father gave me hell, but he bought me another car, the hood of which flew off in a shower of sparks on the New Jersey Thruway. He cleaned up after this too, and for all his bluster he liked my car problems. They became a legend of waywardness, material for you-think-your-kid-gives-you-headaches-well-mine stories that he happily spun out to his friends.

In the spring I joined a fraternity, and from then until I graduated I wasted enormous amounts of time drinking as much as I could and talking about it afterwards. It was the manly thing to do. The other manly things were driving fast and recklessly when half drunk, saying fuck in front of women, bragging about sexual conquests that, in most cases, had not taken place, defending your fraternity brothers against insults and showing your indifference to all academic matters. This was Lafayette's Code of the West. I practiced some of it, the most self-destructive parts, but I went my own way.

I did have academic interests, English and history, but I pursued these so erratically that I failed courses nearly as often as I made A's and B's. I wrote poems, played hockey and began to scatter myself thinly over the college landscape. I finished my first year with a gentleman's B-, and my parents raised a chorus of buckle down, really work hard, get top grades and transfer to an Ivy League school. I gave my oath that I would, but meant not a word of it. Lafayette offered too many chances for me to be noticed *and* be irresponsible for me to consider going anywhere else.

When I arrived home that June, I went right to work for the Tihamer Construction Company. I soon realized that no one knew how to pronounce its name. The drivers who delivered lumber, the clerks at the hardware store and the men who came to pour foundations called it "Tie Hammer" or, getting a big laugh, "Tit-hammer."

Julius Meshberg picked me up every morning, and as we drove to the houses that were already built in Bethel and those under construction in Danbury, he sang my father's praises. As the enterprise spread over three or four towns we got "there" only to drive another twenty or more miles to another job. Late in the summer we worked on a renovation in Washington, Connecticut, that was a good forty-five minutes each way from our base in Bethel.

The three Bethel houses stood ready to be sold. We did rudimentary landscaping and finish work on these. Before a prospective buyer's visit we hustled over to sweep water from their cellars. For some reason (a wet spring, poorly poured concrete, swampy location), all three basements took on water. When it accumulated we swept it out with brooms. At one of these houses we also had to fiddle with the garage door. It didn't fit, but it opened. We beat on it with a hammer until it fit, but then it wouldn't open.

Julius, quiet, humorless and always dressed for work in crisp khakis and a clean shirt, bossed our crew of three. There was John, whose tiny head sat on an enormous body like a cantaloupe on a boulder. He had some carpentry skills. But it was Sal who really knew his stuff. He could wire a house, pour a patio, install toilets or a washing machine, put up Sheetrock, paint, you name it.

He had recently been drummed out of his town's volunteer fire company, an injustice that had him bitching and
moaning all summer. Sal's problems resulted from his affair
with the fire captain's wife. Thinking they'd been seen having
sex in a parked car (according to Sal, she pulled away from
him in fear and he came on her black poodle skirt), she betrayed Sal to the captain, who saw to it that Sal got the heave-
ho. The camaraderie of the company, its musters and annual
carnival, had been the center of Sal's life, and being cut off
from it had embittered him. At least once a day he really
pounded a nail, screaming out that it was her smiling, cunt
face he was beating with his hammer.

Each morning Julius set our schedule. Sometimes he
worked alongside us, but most often he put us to work before
driving off to make the rounds of the other houses and crack
the whip over the subcontractors. His other duty was to track
down Joe Burke, the real estate salesman who had an exclusive on the houses. Joe's office was the white Caddy convertible he drove, and he had a habit of making himself scarce.
Several times that summer he drove up out of the blue to the
site just at quitting time, his arm around a blond, the straw
boater he wore at a rakish angle, and brought a fifth of rye
from under the seat. Julius and John passed on Joe's offer of a
"snort," and after teasing me about being too young for a
man's drink, Joe offered the bottle to Sal, who took a long
pull. Joe had the gift of "blarney," and both Julius and my father described him as a "character" who was a born salesman.
Oh, they knew him to be unreliable, but they also knew how
to handle him. They believed he would be there to turn on
the charm and see the houses they had completed before you
could bat an eyelash. It was all in knowing your man.

This was the summer Mantle and Maris chased Babe

Ruth's home run record. Each day I read of their duel in the *Daily News* and *Mirror,* copies of which were on the lunch counters where we stopped to eat as we drove from job to job. Our work had the pleasures of variety, and plenty of opportunities to loaf over a cigarette and soda while listening to Sal tell another story whose moral was the hell to pay if you followed your dick around town as he had.

We never built a house from the ground up, so there was little sense of accomplishment. But since the odd jobs of work required of us had us going from house to house, I had some idea of the complexities of the business. I knew that when Joe sold two houses that summer, the sales involved bank loans and FHA mortgages. Sal had the impression, which he did not hesitate to express, that Joe played fast and loose with the paperwork.

Joe had another buyer "hot" for one of the houses, but it had to be taken off the market. In a sort of ceremony to mark the house's completion, I climbed a ladder to the gable at one end and attempted to nail a tree branch there. My hammer blow caused the roof to sway. Consternation. I looked down at a stunned Julius, who didn't know what the hell . . . Out came the plans, and up into the attic went Julius and Sal, who soon discovered that someone had neglected to put in a main support beam. Hearing this Joe laughed until he could not stop coughing and had to loosen his tie and dry his eyes.

As usual my father was not forthcoming about his business. I gathered that the FHA provided money when the houses reached certain levels of completion, foundations poured, framework raised, et cetera. From there the finances became intricate, and when I asked my father about them he raced through his explanation. When I did not understand, he treated my questions as argumentative. He always had a short fuse when asked questions about his business, and he jumped at the chance to see me as second-guessing him.

Now that I worked for the company, I brought the work home to our dinner table. From the meals of my childhood, when I tearfully refused to put another cold lima bean in my mouth, to the lectures when I was home from prep school, the dinner hour at our house had always been fractious enough to cause ulcers. If it was a minefield, it was also a court of law. Upon his arrival home my father became the judge to whom my mother presented the evidence of Peter's and my wrongdoing, and my father meted out punishments, usually mild ones. If fatigued by a hard day and more than usually irritated by the tensions at dinner, my father proclaimed, "New rules around here." But it was not long before my brother and I came to see that there were never any new rules, and the calm this threat produced soon dissolved.

My father was less disposed at dinner than elsewhere to open up about his business. What conversation he could not cut off by fiat, he might duck out on by leaving for office hours. When I brought up Tihamer and the personalities of Julius and Joe and let fly my opinions, my mother egged me on. In a reasonably good mood my father might attempt to call the dogs off by slipping into his one comic role, that of Old World paterfamilias. "I want a home where the woman and children," went my father's set speech, "speak only when spoken to and are ready to serve me the moment I walk in the door. When I'm finished, and not before, the three of you can sit down and eat the leftovers then; if there's anything to talk about I'll decide what's to be said."

My mother and I hooted. "Oh, great master" — we salaamed to him, sometimes coaxing a smile. But these were rare evenings. More common were those during which we tried to needle him out of his silence. We might start by gently mocking him for being humorless, he might agree, and the dance continued as we chided him for feeling sorry for himself. We could stay on safe ground, but if Peter sensed the sting in our needle he, who disliked our form of humor, demanded that we lay off.

At this time there was every reason to believe that Tihamer Construction was a going concern capable of making the fortune my father imagined it would. I might be critical of Julius and Joe, but what did I know? Not much, I had to admit. I took it for granted that my father knew what he was doing, and I believed that he did what he did on behalf of the family. I accepted him for the man my mother could fervently describe as "a good Christian, even if he isn't religious, as honest, honorable and ethical as any man" she knew. I never told him I thought of him this way. Our relationship did not admit man-to-man talk. I did not know then that I did not know how to express my affection for him. I had convinced myself that, dinner table friction aside, he knew what I really felt.

Mantle and Maris continued to hit home runs, and I spent my days hauling Sheetrock, picking up after carpenters and plumbers; I spent my nights driving to Norwalk to paint a room in the house of the girl I thought I loved. A girl whose full attention I had a hard time getting and, if I got it, had a hard time holding on to. Part of her allure for me was that she remained just out of reach.

In late August my parents made plans to vacation again in Provincetown, on Cape Cod, and then visit the Verderys in Dennis. They ordered me to join them. I did not want to; I wanted instead to stay home and see Suzanne as often as she would let me. My parents wouldn't hear of it. I would not be left home alone, and they clearly did not think they had to give a reason. I refused to go with them. We quarreled. I argued that I was old enough to stay home alone, that they were treating me like a child, but nothing I said budged them. We skirmished over several days until finally, a few nights before their trip, things came to a head.

At dinner we had avoided the issue. It was now near bedtime. My mother stood in my doorway and asked in a saccharine and provocative tone if I had begun packing. I had a smart retort for her, which my father heard, and he called from their bedroom, "Don't you use that tone of voice with your mother!" The battle joined.

They would not discuss my staying home. Obviously, I was not adult enough, not in control of myself, and could not be trusted to stay home. I argued that I was, and the more heatedly I did so the more they turned my anger against me. If I was so grown-up why did I get so beside myself when I was told I couldn't do something?

"Does this have anything to do with Suzanne?" my mother asked with such mildness that I knew it had to be a trap.

"Nothing."

"That's it. He's in love. That's what's behind all this. He's all wound up because he's in love." My father snorted in contempt. "Look at our boy! Just look at him! He wants to stay home?"

"I'm not in love, and it's none of your business if I am anyway. I want to stay home, that's all. Is that so hard for you to understand?" I wasn't about to admit a thing or give them an inch.

"You can tell your parents. You can tell us," cooed my mother.

"But you can't stay home!" declared my father. "That's final."

"Why? Why can't I? Give me one good reason. You haven't given me one good reason."

"You're the reason. Look at you."

"If it's not about Suzanne, why are you getting so upset? What is there to cry about? If you can't tell us we can't help you."

I had tied myself in knots and I began to sob.

"You know why you can't stay home? You want me to give a reason? Well, go into the bathroom and take a look in the mirror. You're a mess. Come back and ask when you can act like a man."

This undid me. I slammed my bedroom door, as defeated and humiliated as I had ever been as a child. I cried and saw myself, as I had as a child, in a car crash. In my fantasy I lay bleeding on the pavement, my anxious parents bent over me, and to their pleas for forgiveness I said not a word, refusing them comfort for what they had done to me. Ashamed, I cursed my weakness. I was mortified that anyone, that Suzanne, my college friends and teachers, might hear of this fight. I feared that my parents might tell someone, and, worse than this, I feared that I was the child my father told me I was.

Two days later I obediently went with them. In Provincetown I bought my father a cheap leather belt and gave it to him as a gift for the birthday we never celebrated. I meant to hurt his feelings and later, walking along Commercial Street, my mother said that I had.

At the Verderys' my mother asked, in front of everyone at breakfast, if I wanted to call Suzanne and see if she could join us. I wanted to keep a frosty distance from my parents. But I also wanted to see Suzanne and found myself in a bind that I could only get out of by calling her. She came up by train, and the storm between my parents and me blew over.

During my sophomore year I moved into a stone house with a coal-burning furnace down the hill from Lafayette in Easton. Classes got to be too early and too distant. I hardly bothered to get myself up for them. A week or ten days would go by before, late on a Sunday night, guilt overcame me and I'd swear to change my ways, climb the hill bright and early for my biology class and knuckle down to business. My resolve lasted a few days; then I began to skip classes again, and soon I was flunking my courses.

On the mid-October weekend of my birthday, I drove into New York (in the Plymouth convertible, which my father had bought me) and in celebration got drunk enough at Trader Vic's that I had to be carried out by friends. I woke in a friend's Park Avenue apartment with a tropical flower in my hair and more or less sobered up there. I had to get back to Lafayette for an 8:00 A.M. class, and following that I had to drive to Connecticut. Two others had to be back at school as well.

After a few cups of coffee we set out. At 3:00 A.M., in Parsippany, New Jersey, I fell asleep at the wheel and drove the car into a traffic light standard. Dazed, a little bloody but whole, I pushed the car to the side of the road, helped by my unhurt companions, who had been passed out in the backseat. Two high school kids stopped, and we hired them to drive us to Easton. They promised to return to my car and have it towed to a relative's garage.

I made the class and then hitched a ride to Connecticut. My parents had already gone to the Wooster football game, where I was to meet them. I broke into our house and got the keys for my mother's car, which I then drove to pick up Suzanne. By the time we reached Wooster, the game was nearly over. I had not set a precise time for my arrival, but I knew better than to be late on my parents' clock. As we approached I could see that my father was in a slow burn. My mother wore her hurt, why-do-you-do-this-to-me expression, and her face collapsed a little more when she saw the bump on my forehead and the small cuts on my face. They pulled me aside, and I gave them a version of the details that omitted my having been in New York. We had no scene then and there, but our family style demanded one, and this, to Suzanne's chagrin and my embarrassment (at her seeing me grovel before my parents), we had over dinner.

My car did not get taken care of as promised, and within a few days the police called my father, in whose name it was registered. They had found the car, stripped, by the side of the highway. My father called and gave me hell but in a gentle way. As with my other misadventures with cars, he took this one in his stride. I was grateful, and if I paused to think about it I guess I got the message that wrecking your car was not an unmanly thing to do.

After that weekend I got myself up the hill to classes less and less frequently. I did manage to make what I considered a principled stand against mandatory ROTC. Not that I publicly announced the principle when I did not go (as much out of laziness and irritation at having to go) to ROTC classes and drill. I did brag to my friends about what I was doing and to hell with what the Army might do to me.

Months went by without the Army seeming to notice that I was missing. Then a summons came from the colonel in charge. He had just come to Lafayette from Vietnam, which meant nothing to us at the time and would probably have gone unremarked upon had he not married a Vietnamese woman, who looked very exotic in Easton in her native dress. I reported to ROTC headquarters sockless, in clothes I had picked up off the floor of my room, having neither showered nor shaved for three days. A captain paid only enough attention to me to tell me how I must enter the colonel's office, advance to within three steps of his desk, salute and say, "Cadet Corbett reporting."

I agreed to do this, but once inside the man's office I could not and introduced myself by saying, "You sent for me?" The colonel was a ruddy-faced man who wore a red handlebar mustache. On the wall behind him I saw a green plastic water pistol in a frame and under it the name of the fraternity that had given it to him. The colonel looked me up and down. "Do you know what you're doing?"

"What I'm doing?"

"Yes. You're making a serious effort to ruin your career in college. I'll bet your parents have no idea that you are doing this."

"My parents? But both my parents are dead." This popped out of my mouth. I had not expected the question and had not thought that the colonel could easily find out whether or not my parents were alive. My answer surprised him, and he looked down at his desk for some time.

"Be that as it may, you have failed to attend classes and drill and now it is my duty to inform you that you will never wear Army green again while you are here. I expect never to lay eyes on you again. Dismissed."

Once outside I felt proud of myself, proud to have stood up against the ROTC that most Lafayette students ridiculed but few wanted to take on. Since no one knew what had happened, it was easy for me to tell the story in a way that brought me glory.

Most days I arose late, read novels — that year I read most of Dickens — and did not leave the house until time for afternoon classes. As often as not I skipped these to stop at Mama Rosa's Paradise Bar, at the bottom of College Hill. I sat drinking dime' drafts and making small talk with Angelo the bartender. It was winter. By four the place began to fill with fraternity brothers and friends. We drank beer until we decided on the night's next stop. Easton was then a town of drinking clubs (the Young Republicans, the South Side Italian-American Democratic Club), and we usually made our way to one of these hoping for some drunken adventure to take place. In my room I kept a notebook in which, when the spirit moved me, I wrote poems. On its orange cover I had written, "Had I but world enough and time."

I met Beverly that semester, and we wrote letters, but our romance proceeded in a desultory way. Over midyear break I painted a totally unrealistic academic picture for my parents, but my father did not believe a word of it. "He's drinking beer and fooling around. You can forget about his transferring. He's there for the duration if they don't throw him out and into the Army, which, now that I come to think of it, might do him a world of good."

When I returned to school the dean called me in and put me on probation, a status I was somehow able to keep from my parents. I responded by enrolling in the history department's most difficult course, taught by a notorious taskmaster. It was the sort of I'll-show-them act I liked to perform, an act of such obscurity, I did not admit to myself, that it could be lost on anyone and surely did not impress the dean. I made a B in the course but barely passed everything else. When the year ended I was at Lafayette by the skin of my teeth and the administration's sufferance. I was also packing to go to Europe.

That trip took us through seven countries in six weeks. I had not wanted to travel with my family, but foreign countries put us, as it turned out, on our best behavior, and I have pleasant memories of that trip, two in particular. One is the memory of my father bending close to read the texts that interested him in the museums and tourist sites we visited. I had never seen him so absorbed and had not known him to be much of a reader. He did much of his reading on the "throne" while smoking his single cigarette of the day before going to bed. Mika Waltari's *The Egyptian* had occupied him for many months and then came a two-volume paperback history of the papacy. I read enough of this to know that it chronicled every papal crime and scandal in breathless prose. *Catch-22* was the one book my father and I ever talked about. He had seen me reading it, had heard of it and wanted to know if it was any good. I urged it upon him, and he read it in one gulp. When I asked him what he thought of it, he said, "The war I saw was exactly like that. That guy really knows what he's talking about."

In Europe my father showed himself so thirsty for information, a thirst my mother mocked him for with names like Fred Fact and Ted Tourist, that I wondered what he did to satisfy it at home.

The other memory is of a dinner and lunch at the Pyramid Pont restaurant in Vienne, France. I had read about the place and urged it upon my parents so often that they made it a part of our tour, and at a bon voyage party friends gave them a heavy purse of silver dollars, enough so that we could treat ourselves to a meal there.

We arrived just before sunset and were seated on a terrace. High above us the branches and leaves of several thick trees made a roof. We could look out over a lawn to the Roman monument from which the restaurant took its name. White pigeons strutted on the grass.

Ferdinand Pont, pupil of Escoffier and great chef in his own right, had died, but his wife and daughter were there, and so was Vincent, the maître d', whose pleasure it was to serve us. We ate several courses, including a trout in a sauce flavored with chocolate that I can still taste. To top the meal off we asked Vincent, with whom we were by now on intimate terms, to bring us a bottle of expensive champagne. With this we toasted our benefactors. Flushed with the pleasure of the evening, my mother gave her cigarette lighter to Pont's daughter, who had admired it. Before we left, Vincent and my father went over the next day's lunch menu.

Walking back to the Hôtel du Nord down a deserted side street, my mother said she had to pee and, no, she couldn't hold it. While her three men laughingly stood guard around her, she barely had time to take down her corset and send a jet of what must have been pure champagne to the cobblestones.

We returned for lunch the next day, in a brilliant afternoon of hot sunshine. The shade from the trees made the terrace a cool room. We were greeted like the old friends we had become the night before and had another superb meal, which we did not finish until nearly four. After hugs and kisses all around and promises to return soon, we went back to the hotel, where we decided to enjoy our sweet fatigue. I never had a nap like the one I had after sinking into the hotel's goosedown mattress. We came out of our rooms at twilight and walked through the nearly empty town until we came upon a café where we ate a delicious snack of fois gras, cheese and bread and drank white wine. We may never have enjoyed one another as much as we did over that day and a half in Vienne.

It was not until Paris, our last stop, that my father and I had our only serious fight of the trip. We were walking after midnight through Les Halles. Ahead of us two men carrying crates bumped into each other. Curses led to a push and shove. We drew up to them just as one man slugged the other, knocking him to the cobblestones so that his head bounced. When it came to rest, blood flowed from it at once. Instinctively, I knelt to see what I could do for him. My father sidestepped us, helped my mother around the fallen man and walked on. I called after him, and he turned, waving me forward with a sharp motion. I called again, but he kept going. When I caught up with him, and he saw the speech forming on my lips, he stopped me before I could speak.

"Don't say a word! Not a single word! You'll just make a fool of yourself with your silly idealism. I'm not going to help that man and then wind up in some French court with a malpractice suit on my hands. The guy only had a flesh wound. He'll have a headache in the morning, but he'll be OK."

"How do you know?"

"I'm the doctor, that's why you called me. Remember?" He walked on while I stood, stymied and without a retort.

When I caught up to him again I shouted, "That's right, you're the doctor and that man needed help. Isn't it your duty?"

"No, it's not my duty and that's all there is to it. Not here, not now, and I'm not going to say another word about it. Just get down off your high horse and we'll go and have a nice bowl of onion soup."

I shut up and remembered his refusal to stop for the victims of an accident on the Merritt Parkway. I could not have been twelve then. The traffic crept along until finally we passed two wrecked cars. People lay on the grass by the side of the road. I could see blood and hear their cries. "Aren't you going to stop?" I had asked in all innocence. No, he wasn't, and he explained, "You may not understand this, but there are lawsuits for doctors who act like Good Samaritans. I'm not going to take the risk of losing my license while some lawyer gets rich. The ambulance will be along in a minute."

Back at our hotel I picked up the thread again. "What if the guy died? Won't you feel guilty for not helping him? I mean, if it was only a flesh wound why not do what you can for him and leave? You don't have to give your name. He probably doesn't speak English anyway."

"Look, son, I'm going to enjoy myself on the last days of this trip, and you're not going to make me out a bad guy and spoil things. If you can't see what I'm talking about, then I guess you'll just have to go to bed thinking I'm whoever the hell you think I am."

He went to his room, and I went with my brother to ours, where I went over the entire evening, working myself into a self-righteous snit. When he had had enough, my brother told me to shut up and go to sleep.

Another, and more disquieting episode, actually a series of episodes, took place in Paris. My father began to steal things. He had always been a hotel towel and hanger man, but now he began to steal in public. He slipped the mustard pots that sat on café tables, ceramic pots and their wooden paddles, into my mother's purse. We all thought this was amusing. In several bistros he whisked saucers that carried the places' names, and glasses with advertisements in French, into his own coat pocket. Harmless souvenir collecting, but by the time we left Paris he was stealing something at every meal, and this we couldn't entirely laugh off. My mother even asked him to stop for fear that he'd get caught, but he paid her no mind.

Back in the States, he kept up this petty thievery. In Brooks Brothers he asked the salesclerk to show him wallets. When the clerk turned to serve another customer, my father palmed one. According to my mother, he did this several times, as though responding to a dare or wanting to be caught. Once the clerk looked at him hard but clearly did not feel up to challenging a Brooks-suited, mustachioed gent wearing a homburg at whose arm stood a lady in a mink coat.

My parents liked to browse the Pottery Barn, a kitchenware shop, and here too my father stole. He filled his pockets with cordial glasses. On one visit he filched so many that he left the place walking with exaggerated slowness, as if his back ached, in order to keep the glasses from clinking together and giving him away.

We returned home from Europe by boat, my father's cupboard bare. From Paris he had written my grandfather for a loan. I knew this because I had to use my poor French to get my father's money order from the post office. We had spent the money on three-star restaurants, Lasserre and Tour d'Argent. None of us, perhaps not even my father, had an inkling then that we would never spend money like this again.

The weekend after our return I went to Vermont to visit Beverly. I knew when I saw her that I was falling in love. I got home to Connecticut late on the Sunday night the papers carried the headline that Marilyn Monroe was dead, and the next morning, on a few hours' sleep, I returned to work for the Tihamer Construction Company, what was left of it. Julius had an illness he would not talk about and came in only a few days each week. Joe Burke had disappeared from Danbury, leaving angry debtors in his wake. When I went to pick up lumber, the clerk let me have what we needed on credit, but this, he emphasized, was the last time.

Later that week, as Sal, John and I worked around a house in Bethel, the owner of the store where we bought appliances came out to demand money. "I know you don't have a dime and don't know what's what, but tell your old man that I want my money, and I'll see that I get it. Can you deliver that message for me, sonny?" The man who poured the foundations stopped me at a diner with the same message. The Sheetrock man and other subcontractors came by the job to tell me to remind my father that they had to be paid soon.

I dutifully brought this news to him. I hadn't been threatened by any of these men, but their requests had not been polite. I had no idea what to make of things.

"Crybabies"— my father waved my concern and their demands aside. "That's what the construction business is filled with, a bunch of overgrown crybabies."

"But what am I supposed to tell them?"

"Tell them nothing. That's the way this business works and they know it. Someone owes money to me, the FHA owes money to me, and I owe money to the foundation guy and the others, and they owe money to someone else. When the FHA kicks in, they will all get theirs, but tell them nothing. They love to scream bloody murder and threaten you with suits. Only the lawyers really get rich in this business."

"What if they won't give us what we need?"

"Of course they will. They've got money invested in us. Don't make a big deal out of this. All these businesses and all these characters do business in the same way. I know what I'm talking about and you'll see soon enough."

Julius came back to work full-time, but his illness had slowed him down. Now he spent most of his day seeing to the supplies we needed, and I did not have any more contact with the people who claimed Tihamer owed them money. We finished the last Bethel house, and with six weeks to go before school started, I went to work on two new houses, little more than foundations, in Trumbull.

The crew consisted of myself, my fourteen-year-old brother, and an old man named John, who wore a black suit coat over his overalls and lived in a hut in the woods. Mornings, Julius, Peter and I picked him up by the side of the road. John had been a patient of my father's who had fallen on hard times, and he adored my father for giving him work.

John had construction skills, and he completed one task after another, but he gave no orders nor did he ask for help. Peter fell right in behind John, but I did only what Julius directed me to do and then, bored, sat around complaining. John hated this. His loathing came out in a single outburst. He praised my brother and slammed my poor work and lack of respect for my father. "You're a damn poor son," he finished, "and I wish I didn't have a damn thing to do with you."

John's words hurt me into giving a little more to the work, but, really, I couldn't have cared less about doing odd jobs around barren foundations. And besides, I had not been paid, which meant that I had to go to my father for money. This I did not like to do because he would ask me how much I needed and what did I need it for and shouldn't I be saving some for school. The problem was compounded because my father had asked me if I could go without being paid for a while and I had agreed I could.

We were driving in his car, and he spoke as if he actually needed my help. He told me that the FHA money had been slow in coming through and that we had a few problems as he knew that I knew from the workmen coming to me for money. He'd appreciate it if I said nothing to my mother, because she wouldn't understand and it would just worry her, and if I could stand to be paid in a lump sum when I got back to school that would help too. I was grateful for the unusual intimacy and pledged to do what I could to make things easier on him.

By the time I returned to Lafayette, Tihamer owed me $600. I received no lump payment; instead $50 and $100 checks came to me throughout the fall. My father accompanied each of these with a spidery note on a green prescription slip urging me to do well.

Just before I left for school my father suffered a setback he did talk about. Since he and my mother liked going down to Roosevelt Raceway in New York, and having dinner while they gambled, my father leapt at the chance to own a piece of a trotting horse, Edgewood Worthy.

That summer the horse began to race but proved to be a dud, breaking stride several times while we were in Europe. Then the horse improved and ran well enough so that my father's "people," whoever they were, assured him and his partners that good things were in the offing. Edgewood Worthy had a date to run at Roosevelt, so my parents and the other owners decided to make a party of it. My father bet heavily on his horse to win, as did the others. Edgewood Worthy broke in front, and by the three-quarter pole he had pulled away from the field by a few lengths when, as suddenly as if he had been shot by a gun, he broke stride. The fix, my father fumed at dinner the next night, had been in.

"How do you know?"

"The horse broke stride. Three lengths in front, and a sure winner, and the horse breaks stride. The driver knew exactly what he was doing. Someone got to him."

"But don't horses often break stride?" I knew from my father's tone that I would be allowed only one or two more questions before he dismissed me as a smark aleck.

"Yes, but when they do it in that stage of the race . . . well, then you just know things aren't kosher. You see, afterwards we heard this and that around the track, and if what we've heard is on the up-and-up we'll just have to send someone around to the driver and break both his arms and legs."

We laughed at my father's tough-guy tone. He had bragged before about knowing a gangster or two, and we had taken it with a grain of salt. But he'd never said anything like this.

He got the rise out of my mother he had intended. "Bill, you wouldn't!"

"Wouldn't we? We've put a lot of money into this horse. Too much to be treated like chooches. Everyone says the horse has great lines and ought to win races. You saw what I saw, Patsy, what do you want us to do? Thank the guy? There are men who do this kind of thing, and we know how to get in touch with them. Believe me, it's a language that son-ofabitch of a driver will understand."

"Who?"

"Who what?"

"Who are these bad guys you'll get to do this?" I wanted to know.

My father heard my sarcasm. "That, my young friend, is none of your business."

My father's other partners, the ones I was aware of, were a druggist and a salesman for Upjohn drugs, not exactly members of Murder Inc. Were they the ones who knew the leg breaker, or did my father actually know someone in that line of work? Since the subject never came up again, I have no way of knowing what happened. Edgewood Worthy would join the guinea pigs in my mother's tirades.

Returning to Lafayette as a junior on shaky footing, I set things as right as they would ever be and resumed my lopsided, enigmatic course. I seemed to want to play a role in everything, not to excel but to stand out across the board. I was president of the DKE house and openly contemptuous of fraternities. I was a poet and a jock (hockey was my sport) who could be found most evenings in the bars and drinking clubs. I edited the literary magazine, led protests against ROTC, argued school policy with Lafayette's president and dean, and either got interested in the classroom and made A's or did not do a damn thing and got F's.

This last meant that I had to take on more courses than I could comfortably handle. I dealt with this by putting off as much work as I could for as long as I could. Lafayette might have educated me, but I did not allow this to happen. Then I complained about the lack of intensity in classes and the middle-class aspirations of the students and teachers. Now I can see how restless, how impervious to education I was.

I may have acted as if my going off in so many contradictory directions had a purpose, but I knew that I had no idea what I was doing. Not that I admitted to anyone, not even to Beverly, that I was bewildered. Outwardly, my forceful attitudes and opinions projected a convincing assurance. I *was* a rebel, but I needed the Lafayette authorities to approve my rebellion. I proclaimed myself loudly enough to get reactions from others, reactions I needed to define myself. Today I wonder if anyone at Lafayette saw through me as easily as I saw through myself.

It was that fall that my parents' social visits began in earnest. They left an impression each time they came and soon entered the folklore of my friends. My father gave a girl a flu shot after calling her into another room, "Come in here and drop your pants!" During a hockey game he commanded a friend who had taken a stick under his chin to stretch out on the bench and be a big boy while he sutured the cut closed. My friends thought my father a character, and my mother made them laugh.

At first I welcomed, even encouraged, these visits. Most of my school friends would not have wanted their parents anywhere near the school, knowing that they would cramp their style. I thought my parents' visits confirmed that our relationship was now that of adults and equals. But I soon began to grow uneasy. My parents were too eager to charm their way into the hearts of a younger generation. Because I had no way of letting them know my change in attitude without hurting their feelings, I never discouraged their coming. They certainly did not see themselves as poaching on their son's territory, but as with-it parents capable of being chummy with the kids while keeping their distance.

As my parents became more involved in my world, my clandestine rebellion (heavy drinking, dangerous drunken driving and careless neglect of school) intensified. I did not know how to reach the freedom I sought in these acts. Instead, my outward bravado covered an inner guilt that tormented me.

That December my grandparents came by bus and train from Pennsylvania for the holidays. The day before Christmas my grandfather complained of chest pains, dizziness and general discomfort. My father examined him and thought it best that he go to the hospital. Just to be on the safe side. He did not want to go, was in good health, thought it "a damn fool thing to do," but my mother and grandmother insisted and so he went. I drove, nervously and too fast. "Slow this machine down," he asked in a thin voice, sweat on his pale forehead. "We're not late for a funeral."

Christmas Day I sat down to lunch in Beverly's home just as the phone rang. I *knew* it was for me and got up to answer it before anyone else could rise. As I went into the study I knew that my grandfather had died, and that was what my mother, in a voice roughened by grief, told me. I left for home at once.

My grandmother met me at the door and staggered into my arms, calling me by an old pet name, Luke, Luke, and telling me how much my grandfather had loved me. I had no words; I could only hold and pat her. In the living room my mother sat rigid in an armchair I had never before seen her sit in. My grandfather's death had struck her with such force that she was out of place in her own house. She wept, and when she spoke to me bubbles of grief came to her lips. She half rose to meet my hug, and her rigidity vanished. She went limp so that I had to hold her up. "I can see your poppy coming up Center Street from the post office for lunch as clear as I see you right now. I'd run to meet him. I can't get over that I'll never see him again." She collapsed back into the chair.

Stunned by the unexpectedness of my grandfather's death, my father stood silently in the background. Later my mother told me how hard it had hit him. He had been in the hospital on rounds when one of the nurses came with the news. He had been certain my grandfather's symptoms were nothing more than fatigue from his journey to Connecticut. That he might die, had died, was something he could not believe. My grandfather had asked for water, sipped at the offered glass and then turned on his back, sighed deeply and was dead. My shocked father had come home to deliver the news he still could not accept.

I felt blank, empty and very alert. I had never felt such pure emotion from my parents. They were their grief. My grandfather's death, the first in my family, was bound to leave a deep impression on me, but what has marked me most deeply is the reaction of my parents. The absolute had happened, and for the first time in my life my parents' actions and emotions were totally clear to me. I saw that they had no defense against death, and I knew that the truest thing that had happened in my life was taking place. I trace the elegaic note found so often in my peoms to this time.

We went to Jim Thorpe for the funeral, and in the spring my grandfather's burial took place, unattended by anyone in the family, in my grandmother's hometown of Wilkes-Barre. No one in the family ever visited his grave. My grandmother expected to be buried beside him, but after her death twenty years later and the cremation that followed, my mother lost her ashes. She moaned and laughed that she meant to do right, but, well, she had put the urn right where she'd know to find it and when she moved it had just disappeared and no matter how many times she turned things inside out she couldn't find it.

When the school year ended I did not go to work for Tihamer, whose affairs, whatever shape they were in, were now my father's secret. Instead I spun a tale of truths, half-truths and lies so as to spend the summer on 110th Street in New York. The stated purpose was to take two summer school courses at Columbia, but I was much more interested in getting away from home, living with friends and having city adventures. All of which I did, so that I spent little time in class. At the end of the session I showed up for my final exam in Logic, a course I had flunked at Lafayette, then drove through the pouring rain ten straight hours to Beverly's family's summer home in Vermont.

There I moved a desk in front of a window with a view of Caspian Lake, tacked up my now forgotten Dostoyevsky quotation where I could be inspired by it and made a show of going to work every morning. "Work" was "In the Crystal Palace," the novel about a father and son that I had begun three years earlier. This time I studied the dazed August houseflies and daydreamed of Beverly more than I wrote. Actually, I had no plot, and little to say beyond "pity the misunderstood son of the aloof and indifferent father."

My parents had visited me once that summer in New York. My mother called to tell me that a dinner in the city might do my father good. Was he ill? "No, it's the business," she said. "I don't really know. He doesn't tell me anything. But he's not himself. Just don't expect to be taken to an expensive restaurant like before. We don't have that kind of money."

"But I don't care where we eat. What —"

"You don't know what it's been like around here. Just yesterday the sheriff came to the door again with a summons. We're getting to be real good buddies —"

"But that's happened before. You know it's the way the business works. I thought —"

"Your father never says a word. If he owes the money, then why doesn't he pay it? I don't want sheriffs coming to the door. They scare me so that I don't know if I'm coming or going. He's got to get out of those houses, get rid of that zombie Julius and stick to what he knows or we'll be in the poorhouse. I've warned him time and again. It's like talking to a stone."

"Doesn't he tell you anything?"

"We won't have a pot to piss in, mark my words. He comes home, sits down to dinner and the place is like a morgue. The poor guy's worn out."

Typical of my mother, I thought, to exaggerate what was going on and not to tell me what she knew of the actual situation. I knew that in the spring she had given up her gold Cadillac convertible and that she now drove a white Chevrolet coupe. At the time, she had kept after my father for answers, but in talking with me she tended to veer off into dramatics, and I could not tell whether there was serious new trouble or just an increase in her level of frustration with my secretive father. To me, my father was equally uncommunicative. I suspected that in liquidating the Tihamer Construction Company he had found himself in several unpleasant entanglements. He could have let my mother know what was going on; then she might have laid off him. I thought I could see both sides.

They came in on a Thursday, and with Beverly we went to a new eating place on the Upper East Side. It was the restaurant of a cooking school. I had chosen it after reading a review in the *Times* because the place was new and might amuse my parents and because it was cheap.

We entered a black and white room as harshly lit as an interrogation chamber. We could have been pieces on a chessboard. My sorely beset parents needed a big-time New York restaurant, suave mâitre d', leather banquettes, oversized menus and sugar daddies escorting glamorous younger woman to their seats to lift them from their funk. Here the waiters fumbled their tasks, the food tasted experimental and my sullen parents sat like lumps, clearly angry with each other and not about to be entertained no matter how brightly Beverly and I chattered away. Usually, such tensions got resolved in my family by a sudden blowup ignited by me or my mother. Not this night.

When the awkward, sour dinner ended, Beverly and I quickly escaped my parents, who now seemed primed for a fight during the entire hour-and-a-half drive home.

Throughout my senior year, in phone calls, when they came to Lafayette and on visits home, my mother complained about my father. He didn't talk to her; he came in late night after night, the sheriffs came to the door; he wouldn't tell her a thing. If they were to be without a nickel then let it come, but she couldn't take this. I thought she wanted me to take her side, but when I agreed that I knew how difficult my father could be, she defended him. Yes, the construction business had failed, but how could I forget what he had done for us. I had nothing to complain about. After all, I had gotten everything I had ever asked for.

When I rose to this bait, she swerved to speak bitterly about his blaming her for what had gone wrong. At least that was the way she felt when she opened her mouth at dinner and had her head taken off. Peter hardly ate at the house anymore. He'd had enough of their fights.

"Your father tells me to shut up, that it's none of my business. None of my business? I tell him I don't even *know* what business he's talking about. Or he sits there and says it's all his fault until I begin to feel sorry for him and think I can't go on like this after the poor guy. I must sound like a broken record. Well, I tell him if he doesn't want to hear it anymore he knows how to make me stop."

Over Christmas my parents hosted an engagement party for Beverly and me. The following morning over breakfast, they began to wonder if Beverly's parents liked them. Beverly, surprised by this, assured them that they did.

When Beverly left for home and the topic came up again, I began to see that my parents' feelings ran deeper than they had said and that they had forged a bond over this. They charged Beverly's parents with not giving them the time of day. "We do everything for you and that girl," my mother insisted, "but those people act as if we're dirt. Who do they think they are?"

I explained to my parents that while it was true that the Mitchells showed little interest in getting to know them, it was just their way, their lack of social graces. My parents weren't having any of this. They claimed they could tell the difference between formality, even being cold fish, and downright rudeness.

Back at school this theme alternated with my mother's complaints about my father and talk of wedding plans. Oh, did I mind if she picked out Beverly's engagement ring? She could get it wholesale from a patient and knew exactly what would look right on Beverly. I should have said no thanks, but I could see an unpleasant struggle coming. No, I didn't mind.

That St. Patrick's Day I saw for myself why my mother was so concerned about my father. It was a holiday that a group of us from Lafayette traditionally came to New York to drink in Third Avenue bars and raise hell. One St. Patrick's Day I had ridden on the back of someone's motorcycle down a hallway in the Hotel Taft and out through the lobby. In the street the driver stopped, introduced himself as a student at Princeton and roared off. I could not believe I had done such a thing, and did not tell anyone about it for years. When I did, I was met with looks of total disbelief.

This year my parents having gotten friendly with my friends (and because it was my mother's birthday), they joined our party.

We began with Irish coffees at P. J. Clarke's, then crossed the street to Jimmy Glennon's before going uptown to Malachy McCourt's, drinking beer with an occasional shot of Bushmills all the way. We met my parents at the Plaza before, at their urging, we moved on to dinner at the Café Brittany on Ninth Avenue in the Fifties. There were no tables for a party as big as ours, so we waited next door at a Puerto Rican bar, where my father drank shots and beers like one of the boys. He was drunk and cheerful during dinner. After coffee he insisted over my mother's objections that we have one for the road at a nearby Mexican restaurant where he wanted a margarita. This led to a few shots of tequila. Some of the party wandered back to Third Avenue, but my parents prevailed upon Beverly and me to drive home to Connecticut. I asked a few friends to join us.

My tipsy father could not be talked out of driving. My mother sat next to him, and I took the death seat. He seemed in control until we got to the narrow Sawmill River Parkway, where we suddenly swerved left and bounced off the guardrail. When my mother, whose nails were digging into my arm, told him to slow down, he sped up. He meant to terrify us, and when he had, he slowed down. No one said another word until we reached Trumbull. I had certainly never seen him act like this, but he surely was not about to listen to a thing I had to say. In any case, I had troubles of my own.

When I had been dismissed from ROTC, I understood that I would have to make up the credits in Physical Education class. Deciding that I could easily get through what I expected to be no more than a mild nuisance, I let the class go until the last semester. I had not counted on the instructor treating me, and a few others who were there because they had doctors' notes attesting to their allergy to wool, as draft dodgers. I mocked his snarling drill sergeant manner, and soon he had it in for me.

As the semester drew to a close, he took pleasure in reminding me that according to his records I had not swum the required laps or hit the required number of golf balls and my attitude was so bad he didn't see how he could give me a break. I had put something over on ROTC, but I was not going to put something over on him. I had no records of laps swum or balls hit, and I knew the man had it in mind to flunk me. After arguing with him and getting nowhere, I took my case to the dean.

He listened, but after talking to the gym teacher he refused to believe that there was any vendetta against me. If I hadn't done what I was required to do, then I must flunk, no matter how trivial the course seemed to me. If this left me a few credits short of graduating with my class, then so be it. At some point, the dean finished, I had to learn my lesson and take my medicine.

I delayed telling my mother this. I did not want to hear the dying fall of disappointment in her voice, nor did I want to add to her and my father's woes. They were planning to come to graduation, though, so I could not keep the dean's decision from them for long. When I finally called, I began by giving an account of my battle with the authorities, an account that put me in the best possible light. My mother, who had reason to distrust anything I said about school, smelled a rat.

"Well, Mr. Big Shot, this is one time you should have kept your big mouth shut. Those people don't need you to tell them what they've done is right or wrong. You're your own worst enemy."

"Well, it's not my fault that —"

"What's not your fault? That you're not going to graduate? Whose fault is it? It's not my fault. It's not your father's fault."

"No, I won't be graduating, but in this case —"

"It will kill your father. He drags himself around like he's on his last legs, and now this. He's got enough trouble as it is and so do I, but you could care less about that."

"I care. I'm the one who's not graduating —"

"You're the one all right."

If my father had any reaction to my failure to graduate with my class, he did not pass it on to me, at least not directly. When it did come I had to think a second to be certain that I understood exactly what he was saying.

That summer I worked under Jerome Boin at the *Trumbull Times* and, as my father knew, dreamt of being a writer. I also was preparing to wed Beverly in October. One night after dinner we talked about my future. Rather he gave a short lecture on what I would have to do if I wanted to write the great American novel. If I had no way to support myself I was foolish even to consider a career as a writer. He didn't think I expected to have my wife work to put bread on the table. As someone who had to take a bowling course at the University of Bridgeport to attain his college degree, I could hardly expect to overwhelm anyone with my prospects.

Tihamer Construction Company had been, he went on,

his attempt to provide me with a job and someday with leisure to write as I wanted to. "But"— and I remember these words well — "I failed at this and you won't have anything to count on."

My father went off to the office, and I sat feeling sorry for him and then I thought what a shit I'd been not to graduate. I saw that I had let him down the most by not caring about my future. If he had failed so had I. Why couldn't I admit it?

After this conversation I began to defend my father against my mother's attacks. He had already admitted that the company had gone totally bust, what could be gained by harping at him? All that she said about the sheriffs, the idiots he had for partners, the money he had lost, could be true and still, I urged her to see, beside the point. She knew. She knew. But she also knew that the apple did not fall far from the tree, and that I didn't know any more than my father did.

The house became calm for a few weeks. I noticed that the stubble on my father's shaven head was now pure white. I remembered the gray hairs in the beard he had grown on the fishing trip he had taken me on when I was twelve. That wasn't even ten years ago. I realized that my parents had looked the same to me for years and now they had changed. I saw the strain on my mother's face, and my father seemed to have shrunk a little in his clothing.

One night I came home for dinner to find an empty house. My mother's car stood in the garage, but when I called her I got no answer. She was not by the swimming pool. I looked upstairs, calling all the while, but did not find her there. Coming down the stairs I saw her sitting, hunched over, on our front porch, where no one ever sat. I opened the door and called softly. She choked out a response I could barely hear. I made a dumb joke, to which she lifted her head then brought it down into her hands and sobbed.

I went to her, but she recoiled from me. It suddenly came to me that someone — my brother, Beverly, my father — had died. A horrible accident. No, she whispered in response to my question. Nothing had happened. She just did not want to fix dinner. She had been shopping in the supermarket when she began to bawl. She had, she said, a hot flash, but I wouldn't know what that was and anyway all that I cared about was her seeing to dinner. "How much"— she looked at me tearfully — "do you and your father think I can take?"

I coaxed her to come inside and got her a glass of water. Seated at the kitchen table, she wiped her tears away, embarrassed by them. "You men"— she looked right into my eyes — "none of you know a damned thing. If I didn't make dinner every night you and your father and brother wouldn't know how to boil water. I even had to pick out the engagement ring you gave Beverly."

"But I thought you wanted to do that." She knew this had become a sore subject between us. "You did that before you even told me you were going to. You're switching everything around now."

"Don't you dare criticize me!" Her lip trembled. "Not one more word." She slapped her palm on the table and left the room. I knew better than to follow her upstairs.

When my father came home and I told him what had happened, he used the phrase "change of life" to explain it. "It comes and goes," he continued, "and there's not much for us to do except let her alone and not make matters worse. You must have noticed her up and down moods."

"No," I replied. "Well, yes," I corrected myself, "now that

you mention it I have, but I thought it had to do with the money and —"

"That too. Let's wait for your brother, then go get something to eat. I'll go upstairs and see how she's doing."

I never saw my mother in such a state again. As she got more and more involved in our wedding, it seemed to restore her to her old self. She liked to think of Beverly as a protégée, and when Beverly drove up from Old Greenwich to go shopping with her my mother was delighted. She had had this relationship with other young women, whose hair she dyed and whose clothes she helped picked out. According to her, Beverly could benefit from "doing something with herself," and my mother eagerly took on the role of coach.

She also returned to the theme of Beverly's parents not treating her and my father with respect, and she brought my father with her. "They act as if we're not good enough for them. We may not have their money, and we don't come from Greenwich, but we've had them up here, had that big engagement party for you with all their friends invited, and we've not been inside their house for so much as a glass of beer. Don't you think there's something wrong with these people that they're treating your parents this way?"

I explained that the Mitchells did not mean anything by this, but that seemed to support their view and only served to get me in deeper. I talked it over with Beverly, who prevailed upon her parents for an invitation to dinner. This took place at the Mitchells' country club and proved only that the two couples had nothing in common except a wedding.

The dinner did not curb my parents' enthusiasm for seeing themselves as victims of snobbery. They kept up their grumbling. I began halfheartedly to agree with them, if only to avoid an argument and, in part at least, because I had begun to see their point. The Mitchells did seem cold to them. Then an unpleasant incident occurred.

As the day of our wedding neared, Beverly's father, Sprague, began to forget long-arranged plans, and several times in everyday situations he spoke incoherently. He was deaf, and had always zoned out to a degree, but this was worrisome. While watching a baseball game on TV with him, I realized that he thought we were watching the Duke Snider and Jackie Robinson Dodgers of the nineteen fifties. He then began to pick the cigarette butts from the ashtray in front of us and laboriously smooth them out. When finished, he piled the butts neatly in an end table drawer. He saw me looking and with great solemnity said that he really ought to save them for Beverly's wedding.

He seemed to be losing his mind. Beverly, her mother and I decided that we could not call the family doctor for fear that a visit from him would alarm Sprague. We thought my father could stop with my mother for a drink and, if not make an actual examination, perhaps pick up some clue that might explain the man's strange behavior. My father agreed to this plan and duly came down with my mother.

That evening Sprague appeared dull and listless, and when my father suggested they go upstairs and take a look at what was the matter he did not object. In fifteen minutes my father came downstairs with a few reassuring words for Beverly and her mother. He thought the symptoms had no obvious physical cause and would most probably pass.

Upstairs Beverly's mother found her husband in tears. He told her my father had hectored him to snap out of it, come to his senses and quit babying himself. My father threatened that if he didn't stop acting like a crazy person he would soon be treated like one. It was a few days before I found out what my father's "examination" had consisted of.

I immediately went to him, and he did not deny that he had given Sprague a talking-to for his own good. He made no attempt to disguise his contempt for the man. I could not help but see that my father had humiliated Sprague on purpose, had, in fact, taken his revenge on the man. But as angry and ashamed as this made me, I did not call him on what he had done. Using the tensions already surrounding the wedding and my own jitters as an excuse, I took the coward's way out. Sprague's condition, perhaps an attack of anxiety brought on by the wedding, improved on its own, and within weeks he had returned to normal.

On October 3, 1964, Beverly and I were married before hundreds of guests, many of whom we barely knew, in an Old Greenwich church we had first set foot in the night before. We were really little more than characters in a drama dominated and controlled by our four parents. We did what we were told. So eager were we to put the entire event behind us that Beverly had her wedding dress off before she realized that she had not thrown the bridal bouquet. Back on went the dress, and the bouquet flew through the air.

The last photographs I have of my father are from our wedding. I can read no particular emotion in his face. He might be posing for a passport picture, but his posture, drawn up, chest out-thrust, is that of a hussar. He is a proud man, but it is impossible to tell if he is taking pride in the event.

We honeymooned for a week in Vermont and then drove to Cambridge, Massachusetts. Based on a long weekend in Boston and Cambridge the year before, we had decided to live there. We knew only Beverly's former roommate and in a few days had found an apartment near hers, not too far from Central Square. My parents drove a car full of our possessions up to us.

In all household tasks my father held the rank of general. His loathing of the work caused him to demand total control. During my childhood every home repair and necessary maintenance chore had been a trial. When we worked together it was a disaster. At ten I held a metal stake for him to drive into the ground with a sledgehammer. When I did not hold it steady enough or understand exactly how he wanted it done from the movements of his hand, he saw red. The hammer came down, catching enough of my finger to smash the skin and send blood flying. He helped me into the house, where, while he administered first aid, I fainted.

Our move into the Harvard Street apartment produced the usual peevish sighs and harsh orders but no major upset. My father and mother's ongoing battle seemed to take most of his energy and hers as well. This was not a pitched battle but more like a persistent stomachache or thunder that cannot bring rain. The decline in their fortune had been steady for the past two years. On this weekend they slept on the floor of our apartment rather than spend money on a motel room. I did not know until my mother called me from Trumbull upon their return that there had been a more direct cause for their tight-lipped acrimony.

My father had lost our house. That, she told me, was the way she saw it, but he insisted that if they let it go to the bank there was a way they could pay off some of their debts when the house sold. She had given up fighting him on this. What was she to do? The anger in her voice had been thinned by weariness. I gave her some words of comfort, but the truth is that I felt there was nothing I could do but listen to her, and, I admitted to myself, I had grown weary of it.

Before winter they moved into a split-level house in a development across the road from the farmer's fields my father and I had tramped through after our one and only squirrel hunt. The Stonehouse Road house stood vacant as somehow my father held the bank off from foreclosing on it. When we drove past it on a visit to my parents, I did not feel even a twinge of regret that it would never be my home again. A real estate agent's For Sale sign had been driven into the front yard. I could only wonder at my lack of feeling.

In May, Beverly and I hosted a going-away party for our friends Jim and Linda Harrison, who were returning home to Northern Michigan. My mother, who had met Jim when he stopped in Trumbull for dinner, came up that weekend without my father. He had taken a business trip.

During that raucous, drunken party I began to talk with my mother about my grandfather. Half drunk, I started to weep as I remembered him. It was now that she told me how stricken my father had been at my grandfather's death, and how it had shaken his faith in himself as a doctor that he had not guessed the severity of my grandfather's condition.

"Your grandfather liked your father," she continued, "but he would have hated what he's done these past few years. Your grandfather knew how to manage money, and he talked everything over with your Nanny Mench. He left her very well taken care of. Not like your father, who's put us all up shit's creek."

Later that spring we visited my parents for a second time in their new house. After dinner on the first night, my father's lawyer and another friend came over to play poker. For years my father, by his own account a shrewd player, had convened a regular poker night at our old house. During the move he had sold the table covered in green baize with its rectangular wells in front of each player for chips and round wells for drinks. I had never seen him actually play the game, and to make a social event of it was entirely out of character for him.

I held good cards throughout, played them decently and delighted in taking pots from my father and his friends. But it was low stakes, kitchen poker and we talked as we played.

"Why aren't you driving your car?" my father asked me as if he had just that minute noticed I had driven up in another.

My car was a Ford station wagon. I had lent it to a friend so he could move into his new house more easily. I explained this to my father, who knew the friend. It was his chin he had stitched during that Lafayette hockey game.

"Lending your car"— he snorted, shaking his head at the thought that he had fathered a boy as dim as me — "lending someone your car is like lending them your wife!"

"What?"

"Just deal," he commanded, "just deal the cards."

It was on this weekend that we had our first go-round about Vietnam. The subject had come up on the television news, and since I had long ago formed strong views, I sounded off. I knew something about the war from Lafayette's corps of ROTC officers, in particular a captain who drank beer with us, and several of whom had served there. In the summer of 1963 I had taken part with friends from Columbia in a demonstration against the war that circled Times Square. Our signs bewildered most of the passersby, who hardly knew what we were demonstrating against. I told my father that if I had the bad luck to be drafted I would not go to Vietnam.

"If you're called you'll go. That's what I did, and that's

what you'll do because that's what a man does. You're talking like you have a paper asshole. When your country calls you'll go."

"I won't. Wait and see." The gorge rose in my throat.

As usual we did not discuss a subject or even really argue about it. Instead I found myself in a battle of wills with nothing to refute and no argument to make.

"Oh yes you will. I didn't want to go. Do you think I wanted to go and leave your mother and maybe get killed? Of course not. But that's what a man must do or be a coward. You'll want to be a man just like the rest of us."

During dinner as we made small talk, my convictions began to seem flimsy to me. I mean, if I could do nothing more than assert them . . .

A few months later I gathered with a group of strangers on Boylston Street to listen to a car radio as President Johnson ordered 80,000 American boys to Vietnam. By this time the war was upon us in earnest, and my passionate arguments against it would never reach my father, who was long gone.

Over that summer, in all her phone calls, my mother repeated her concern for my father: his loss of weight, the way his clothes hung on him, his not being able to get to sleep after being out on calls until all hours and his soldiering on in the face of the pack of wolves at their door. Then her tenderness turned to rage at his stubborn refusal to let her know exatly where they stood. She didn't even know why their house had not been sold. "It's not the money I mind," she continued, "it's that he never told me a damn thing that he was doing, and he still doesn't. Some nights when he's asleep next to me I want to take a hammer and bash that bald head of his. Knock some sense into him. Then, oh I don't know, I get to feeling guilty as hell, you know, and want to hold him in my arms and make everything better, and I don't know what to do."

These calls came so frequently and their content was so similar that I became inured to them. My mother really wanted no more than for me to listen. This I did, but with less than total attention. The details of what she said did not change, and I did not register an unfolding narrative so much as a single, steadily held complaint.

In September, Beverly and I moved to Hanover, on the South Shore where we lived with friends before finding our own apartment on the top floor of an old house. My mother came to visit soon after we had moved in.

She could never hide anything. One look at her told me things had changed for the worse. My father had come to her, she said, and confessed that he had made a mess of their life, that he no longer wanted to practice medicine and that all he wanted was to leave her and go away. He had no idea where he would go or what he would do when he got there or how long he planned to stay, but he was determined to go and nothing she said could hold him. She was not sure she believed everything he said, but she feared he might "do something to himself."

"Maybe you should come home and talk to him. Maybe you can talk some sense into him."

"If that's what you want, then I'll go back with you." I had just quit a job in an advertising agency and planned to let Beverly's salary support me while I stayed home and wrote.

"Well, maybe it's not time for that yet. I wish I knew. What can you tell him that I haven't said?"

"Is he planning to leave or not? You've just changed your mind so quickly I don't know which way is up. Has he told you when he plans to go? I mean, what day?"

"No, no." She was exasperated with me. "He doesn't really want to go anywhere. He doesn't want to be where he is, and I can't blame him. All our friends know. He doesn't want to face them and neither do I. I hate it when people look at me in the stores when I go out, and it must be worse for him."

"Look at you how?"

"We owe everybody, everybody, and we wouldn't owe a goddamn cent if he'd listened to me in the first place and not gone into business with that Julius Meshberg and those others. What did he know about houses anyway? And then he just began throwing good money after bad. I get so mad I don't care if he goes away and never comes back."

"You don't mean that."

"Of course I mean it, and I don't either. But none of this is my fault. I'm good with money. None of this would have happened if he'd let me take care of things."

Into the night my mother skipped from one subject to another. I had to piece together what she would have called "a blow-by-blow description." I knew she could only be this agitated if my father actually did intend to leave her; then she changed her tune and I wasn't so sure. One minute she wanted me to come down and talk to my father, the next minute she despaired that anything could be done to stop him, and in another breath she had already let him go, to hell with him.

Late that night, Beverly having gone to bed and my mother finally having followed her, I drove over to talk with a friend. I told him what I knew for certain and recounted my mother's fears. He advised me against running down to talk with my father. Perhaps my mother was exaggerating, but in any case she obviously did not think the time was ripe. I might make matters worse by butting in. What did I really know of my father's affairs anyway? If I got myself in the middle I might become the issue, and what good would that do?

"If you go, what do you plan to say to your father?" he asked.

I admitted that as of the moment I had no idea. I explained that I knew my father probably did not want to hear another word about his businesses. "I guess I'll ask him why he is going to leave and then talk him into staying. But if he doesn't want to stay with my mother, I doubt he'll even consider staying just because I want him to."

After another drink I drove home to bed no clearer about what course of action I should take. The next morning my mother returned to Trumbull. I heard nothing from her for a week and had begun to feel that the crisis must have passed when she called. In a flat, dull voice she told me that my father had "one foot out the door" and if I expected to do any good I had to come at once.

Later that afternoon he met me at the Bridgeport train station. In the car I began to question him about his plans. He cut me off before I could say more than a few words.

"We'll talk about that at home with your mother and brother." He had dark rings under his eyes, and since he had not shaved his skull for a few days, there was a horseshoe of gray stubble around his bald dome. His shirt did look a few sizes too large, as if he had borrowed it from a bigger man. We drove on in silence.

When I came through the kitchen door, my mother gave me a look that said things were hopeless. We went into the family room to talk. My brother turned off the television show he had been watching. As my father, looking directly at me, began to tell me that he was leaving my mother, she got up and walked across the room saying, "I'm not going to sit still and listen to that again, Bill. I'll be in my room. You come and tell me what this damn fool has to say for himself."

I urged her to stay.

"Let her go if she wants to," my father said in a calm, patient voice. "She's already heard what I have to say, and she just won't listen. You will be able to understand what I'm saying and convince her that I mean it. Your brother understands, don't you, Peter?"

Peter, seated on the couch next to my father, nodded yes.

My father cleared his throat and held his hands open in front of him. "I simply do not love your mother anymore, and I've told her this in as many ways as I can. She doesn't believe me, but it is the truth. I am going to leave her. She thinks there is something you can say to me that will change my mind, but I'm telling you that there is nothing, nothing that will change what I am going to do. What you ought to do is be a good son and think about what you can do for her. My mind is made up. I am going away."

"But where will you go? Will you give up your practice? Will you —"

"You can think of it as a vacation. I don't really know where I will go, but I think you can already see that I am going. I may be gone for a few months, maybe longer. About the practice, tomorrow you and I will go to see Vinnie Adley, and he'll go over in more detail what I've already gone over with Peter and your mother. I've made all the arrangements."

His speech had slowed as if he thought I might have trouble comprehending what he said. "Your mother will get money from the patients when they pay the bills my secretary will send out. There's the kidney dialysis machine to sell and the office stuff. She'll have this house."

"What about the old house? Will she —"

"The bank has that, but she'll get something from it when they sell it. Adley will see to that when the time comes. Just listen to me, follow what I am telling you and let me finish. Ruby will bill all the patients who owe money. It's a substantial sum, ten thousand at least. As that money comes in, it will go straight into an account for your mother. The kidney machine is worth a few thousand dollars, and the office furnishings are practically brand new. Your mother will have her car."

"When did you decide?"

"Decide what? To leave her?"

"That you didn't love her. I mean, she told us you broke the news to her before she came to visit us, but she never said that you said you didn't love her."

"It doesn't matter when I decided. You can ask Peter what it's been like around here. You've been in Boston and have no idea but what she's told you. The point is that I no longer love your mother. She finds that hard to believe. I understand that. These things don't happen for any one reason you can put your finger on. If you can't understand that now, you will have to understand it in time."

"But what's that got to do with not being a doctor any more?" My head had begun to spin. The speech I had prepared to deliver had vanished from my mind. I had only questions to ask, which he answerd in a painstaking way as if he were speaking to a child.

"I may well be a doctor again, but it's not going to be here. There's nothing left for me in this town."

"But after twenty-five years, you don't just leave your practice —"

"Listen to him." Peter spoke his first words. "Can't you hear what he's saying?"

My father shushed Peter. "He's got to ask these questions

for himself. Let him do it his way. He hasn't heard my side before." To me he said, "I'll sit here as long as it takes for you to see exactly what I'm talking about. Now what part of it don't you understand?"

He took me through it again, repeating what he had said but adding no new details. He finished and we sat in silence. There was nothing more to say. He had told me what he wanted me to hear.

I went into their bedroom to speak with my mother. "He just keeps telling me that he is leaving you because he doesn't love you anymore. What can I say to him?"

She sat in her bed propped up by pillows. An open magazine lay on her chest. "Oh, I know that's what he keeps saying. Let him go then. I don't think he will go, but this is driving me crazy. If he goes, we'll all get a moment's peace. If that's what he wants to do, the hell with him. I can't take this anymore." She began to weep.

I returned to my father and brother. It was long past the dinner hour. My mother had told me she was not hungry. We drove off to a roadside hamburger stand. I wanted a drink, and I wanted to be alone as I drank it and thought things over. My father ordered me a hamburger. When it came I couldn't eat it and let it sit on its paper plate.

Back at home, my brother said he was going to visit a friend and my father had an errand to run. I looked in on my mother, who had fallen asleep with her light on. I poured myself a bourbon and water and called Beverly to report that my coming had been a waste, that I had listened but not really gotten a word in edgewise.

Then I sat in front of the TV with another drink. Midnight came. I replayed what my father had said and did not see an opening for me. He meant to leave. That was that. I went to bed and heard my brother come in just before I fell off to sleep.

In the morning my father sat in the kitchen, already dressed, drinking his coffee. Peter had gone to school, and my mother did not want to leave her room. I had some juice and a cigarette. For once my father did not nag me about smoking. My mother came in for coffee, and my father merely nodded in her direction. When he went to the bathroom she told me that he had not come home last night.

My father and I had made the drive down Main Street to Bridgeport thousands of times. On this early autumn day a dull sun shone through the cloudy sky. My father slowly repeated the facts and figures he had stated before. This served to deepen the fog in my mind. So many patients owed so much money and so much more money would come from the sale of this and the sale of that and your mother has, you know, a little nest egg. "It will probably be a good thing for her to go back to work," he added, "but she'll be able to think about that later and do it when she's good and ready."

We parked in a lot near the train station. It dawned on me that I had arrived only yesterday, and that this morning I had kissed my mother good-bye and would leave for Boston after our meeting with Adley.

We walked the few blocks to his office. As we got off the elevator on his floor and I looked down the empty corridor, my father stopped and put a hand on my arm. He wanted a minute alone with his lawyer. "I hope you won't mind waiting in the hall." He said this as if asking a favor. Without hesitation I agreed.

I could not see through the pebbled glass of Adley's office door nor could I hear a word of what was going on. I assumed that Adley had a secretary and that my father and he must be in another, further, office. I lit a cigarette and traced with the toe of my shoe the green abstract pattern in the floor's black linoleum. Finished with the cigarette, I walked the length of the corridor, passing other offices in which I could hear nothing. I ground out my butt in the smooth sand of an urn. I felt as bored and restless as I had waiting in my father's car for him to return from a house call. I was debating whether I could just walk into Adley's office when my father opened the door.

Beyond the tiny waiting room where no secreteary sat was a small office. Vinnie Adley, tall and black haired, whom I had always liked for his dry sense of humor and because he liked me, rose and took the hand I offered. My father took a chair by Adley's side, and I sat facing both men. I might have been in a job interview.

"Tell the boy what we've been talking about, Vinnie."

And Vinnie dutifully explained that my father had given him power of attorney. Then he repeated the facts and figures I had already nearly memorized. He spoke as if reading from a script. When he finished, he smiled and asked if I had any questions.

I asked something about the power of attorney more because I thought I should have a question to ask than because I really cared about the answer.

Adley told me what I wanted to know and then asked about Beverly. We made small talk. For no reason I suddenly remembered that at a party at his house he had played a tape of Art Linkletter telling dirty jokes, saying shit and fuck with gusto at a Friars' Club roast. I could see Beverly and me standing in the basement of his house. I asked about his wife and children. His answer filled the time until I had to go and catch my train.

My father and I walked back the way we had come, and I got my bag from his car. As we walked to the train I didn't know what to say. Outwardly, my father was as calm as he had been since my arrival. We had done our business. I thought I really ought to have something to say, but no words came to me.

I boarded and standing on the metal steps turned to shake my father's hand. He sent his best to Beverly. I wished him well. Looking down at him, shrunken in his white shirt and black suit, I saw how small and tired he had become. Defeated, diminished — I loved my father. As the train pulled out of the station, he gave me a half salute and turned away. I felt something in my hand and looked there to see the two twenty-dollar bills he had passed me in his farewell handshake. When I looked up he was gone.

PART II

THREE DAYS LATER I was on the train back to Bridge-port. I wore a suit and a hat so as to appear older than my twenty-three years. In the smoking car I tried to concentrate on Faulkner's *The Hamlet*. I'd read a sentence or two, then drift into thinking about my father having done what he'd said he'd do, and then the thought spun its wheels. I had packed for the two weeks I thought I might need to stay in Trumbull.

The landscape sped by just as it had when we had driven as a family down the Merritt Parkway to Manhattan. I was that boy again in the backseat with my brother listening to my parents talk while amusing myself with the image of a long blade, a sickle, attached to our car slicing down the trees we passed. Was it on one of those trips that I'd first heard my father say, "I want to be able to look at my face in the mirror when I shave"?

I lit another cigarette. My mouth already tasted dead from them. My first year at Wooster I went to the Danbury Fair with a pudgy, blond boy. Douglas Home. When he closed his mouth, rods from his elaborate braces dug into his soft lips. I suddenly saw these lips again. That day I told Home to call me "Doc." He tried, but kept forgetting, and I berated him.

"That's Doc!" "Not Bill, Doc!" He couldn't learn to do it, and I never tried to use the name again.

Several sailors got on at New London and joined me in the smoking car. I looked again at the words in my book but could not concentrate. I looked up at the passing blur of fall leaves. For a long time I sat dumbly, thinking nothing.

My mother and brother were at the home of Paul Goulding, an undertaker, and his wife Elvira, old friends, who had known nothing of my father's plans until my mother's call telling them he had left. Louis Kaye drove me to their house.

In their living room my mother rose from a chair to greet me with open arms. She had on dark glasses. She wobbled on her high heels as she came toward me, and I could see that her lipstick was smeared. I had never before seen her wear dark glasses indoors. As we hugged she wailed, "Your father packed a picture of Apricot. He had tears in his eyes. Can you believe it? A picture of the *dog,* and I felt sorry for the bastard. I even helped him pack, and now her."

Her was Gloria. I had met her once or twice, did I remember? A black-haired woman, short, good figure. Not your father's type at all. She ran convalescent homes, had met your father years ago in one of them. I thought I could picture her wearing a full-skirted white dress, a ball gown. She had had the hots for my father. They kept a place in Milford at the beach. That was where my father must have gone on his errand the last night I had been at home. Louis knew about her, but not how long it had been going on or how serious it was. They had been surprised screwing in one of the rooms in the old-age home. And once Trumbull cops had come upon them in a lovers' lane. She had a husband, who had already called the house looking for her. He had no idea where she had gone.

Where had they gone? We didn't know. We did know that they left Thursday after he put the note on his office door. Someone in the real estate office across the hall had seen him tack the note to his door, and he asked where my father was going. "Read the note" was all my father said to the man he had talked to every day for over ten years. The man read, "I have gone to further my education." My father stood beside him in tears.

"The old boy doesn't have the sense of humor to mean that as a joke," my mother interrupted Louis's narrative.

"After your mother called you, Paul here drove her to Brooklyn, where she remembered there had been $10,000 on deposit. Your father must have forgotten it. She got that out of the bank, and it's damn lucky she did because as far as we can tell there's not another dime anywhere."

"But he put Adley in charge!"

"He lied to you! Adley didn't know a damned thing until your father called him that morning to make the appointment you went to. He said what your father told him to say, and he's one sorry bastard right now."

"I waited in the hall." Everyone was talking at once. "I waited in the hall," I repeated to all of them.

"You waited in the hall," Louis spoke as if reciting, "while your father told Adley that he was leaving with Gloria and gave him power of attorney over what we still don't know. The bank had already foreclosed on the Stonehouse Road house, but your mother didn't know that. He didn't tell you, did he? No. Of course he didn't. None of us knew. They'll auction it off in a month or so, and your mother won't see a red cent from that."

"The day he left," my mother spoke, "he took those coins, those Indian head whatchamacallits, twenty-dollar gold pieces your poppy gave to you and Peter. We were there in the kitchen. He had his bags packed. He dropped one of the coins on the floor, and wouldn't you know it rolled under the stove. This will kill you. I helped him move the damned stove and watched like a perfect asshole as he dug around under there until he came up with the coin."

"He could have asked for money from me," — Paul sounded wistful, sad to have been left out — "but he never did."

"Consider yourself lucky," snapped Louis.

By the end of that day we knew that my father and Gloria were on their way to Europe and that his last words to Beverly had been "Things are not what they seem." Not what they seem? What things? What isn't what it seems?

In the days ahead we chewed over those words as we learned that save for the Brooklyn account all the others had been stripped, even a savings account in Newtown that held money given by my grandparents for Peter's education. We expected the long-outstanding bills from subcontractors, lumber companies, hardware stores, appliance wholesalers but not several overdue loans from banks in Danbury and Bethel. My father had long since cashed in his life insurance policies, and now we learned that during their move he had, without my mother knowing, sold off his collection of shotguns and rifles, a coin collection and the stamp collection I had put together as a boy. We soon learned that he had borrowed from several of his patients. A friend called, breathless with the news that my father had been turned down just before he left by a Hungarian credit union. We laughed at the man's pleasure in bringing us the news.

And we laughed again when a man who gave his name as Lefty called to ask if the story was true that "the doc has skipped town." When I told Lefty that it was indeed true, he asked, "Has your father made any provisions for his creditors?"

"Did he borrow money from you?" I asked.

"I would not call it a loan. Let us say that we had an arrangement."

I said that my father had made no provisions, and that there wasn't a dime on hand to pay off any of his debts. Lefty reacted with equanimity, and he never called again.

In telling my mother about his call, I imitated Lefty's cultivated tone and the way he drew out the word "arrangement."

"He sounds like something straight out of *Guys and Dolls,*" she said, as she began a fit of laughter that ended in tears.

From a druggist friend we heard that my father was "in" to the loan sharks for upwards of $40,000, but he knew of no Lefty. He did take the trouble to warn us solemnly that if my father stayed over in Europe he might have hell to pay. The men he had borrowed from did not take deadbeats lightly.

Had my father been involved with the underworld? He liked to give the impression that he knew more about mobsters than he could let on. Louis thought this was all show, had never heard even a rumor about my father and the mob and didn't believe it now. Loan sharks? Why not? The act of a desperate man, but not necessarily a criminal. Perhaps Lefty was a grifter trying to work the situation to his advantage.

My mother thought to call my father's brother Frank, from whom our family had been estranged for over fifteen years. It was from him we learned that my father and Gloria had been at his New Jersey home before their flight to Europe. In fact, they had been there on the weekends my mother had come to Boston alone and they had, over the past two years, driven down for numerous overnight visits. Even Ma Corbett had reconciled with Frank, after years on the outs, and joined them. The guileless Frank poured this out. He couldn't believe that we had no idea of what had been going on. Nor could he believe that his brother had kept from us his European vacation and his ultimate destination — Baghdad.

Baghdad! This floored us. Sultans wearing shoes that turned up at the toes. The Arabian nights. Veiled women and men in flowing robes. Baghdad!

And then I remembered an evening at the restaurant of my father's fellow Hungarian Bill Ratzenberger. They had been talking about Arpad the Hun Killer, whose two-handed broadsword had split like kindling wood the Mongols who rode small, hardy horses and carried their diet of dried meat under sheepskin saddles. Around this campfire of dessert plates and coffee cups, my father made his remark about Arabs.

"The Arab will rule the world." He stated it as a matter of fact. Challenged, he explained how easily the Arabs could shut off their oil.

"Their oil?" His audience guffawed. It was the late fifties. My father met their laughter with smug silence.

Then I remembered the months when his bathroom reading had been a paperback copy of *The Saracen Blade*. Had this tale of derring-do during the Crusades contributed to his vision of Arab hegemony and awakened a desire of Levantine adventure? Unlikely, but at some point he and Gloria must have researched Baghdad. That they traveled there at such leisure suggests a job awaited him, or at least prospects. The city was obviously part of their plan.

But their destination did not disturb my mother as much as learning of my father's and Gloria's visits to Frank's house. And Ma Corbett to boot! A regular family reunion! She could not get over her ignorance of the affair, of how long it had gone on, how much time she had had to catch on but hadn't, how sneaky they had been and how good at it. Nor could she forgive herself for feeling sorry for him. He had lost so much weight, worked so hard, looked so dog tired, did all he could to get them out of the hole while all the time scheming and lying his way to Milford and New Jersey to be with his other woman! How could her friends believe that she didn't know? She could hear tongues wag: "How could Patsy not know? I mean, two years." He had destroyed their life together, and now she knew that while he was doing it he had been making a fool of her.

And what a fool he had played me for. The kidney machine, spoken of by him as if it were instant cash? It was two years old, and brought only a few hundred dollars. My father owed back rent on his office. As a favor to us the landlord wrote it off, but only after he confiscated the office equipment and furnishings, including the local churches' commemorative plates that my father had displayed on his waiting room walls.

It did not take long for it to become apparent that little of the money patients owed my father would be forthcoming. He really had no reason to expect that patients he had abandoned would pay their bills, and we shouldn't have either. Why had I not thought of this when he went over and over this source of income? He couldn't have believed what he told me. Or was he so deluded, so bent on achieving his plan, that he believed everything he said because he had to convince me? When it came to light that my father had kept no records for the past few years, we all learned that his patients had been doubly betrayed and, though a few felt my mother deserved the money they owed and paid up, most found good reasons not to.

For weeks patients continued to call in disbelief. First, they could not believe that my father had actually left town. Then they could not believe that we had been as ignorant as we said we were. They called to get their records and were amazed and often outraged that we had none to give them.

A flurry of calls came nearly six months later, when the rumor that my father had returned ran around town. Many were eager to believe that it was true, that the only doctor they had ever had was back. They stopped my mother when she shopped in the supermarket and praised my father, vowing that he was the best doctor they had ever had and asking what she heard from him.

Everything about these encounters angered my mother. People did not want to hear her story. Hell, she had no idea where he was. Baghdad? They couldn't believe that. How dare they think that she had any contact with him. They had lost only a doctor, and could use the phone book to find another. She had been the one to lose everything, and some of them were so crude they couldn't even think of how much she had suffered. Why did they think she wanted to hear about what a wonderful doctor he had been? If he was so damned good, why wasn't he still there?

On a brilliant November Saturday morning, I stood in the small crowd scattered around our empty Stonehouse Road living room. No one there recognized me, or if they did they kept it to themselves. The auctioneer led us through the chill and empty rooms. When we came to the cell-like room that had been mine, I was surprised to feel nothing at all. I searched the windowsills for the places where I had carved my name, but even the sight of my crooked "Billy" carried little impact. I thought I ought to feel something more than this failure to feel anything. I had grown up in this room.

Something must be wrong with me, some emotional deficiency. How could I anonymously enter these rooms and blandly look around as if I might have a bid in mind?

Then we went down into the cellar. Here I peered into the gloom of the crawl space that ran under the living room. On its earthen floor, furry white mounds blazed up. Mounds of what I alone knew to be moldering dog shit. When banished to the cellar, this was where Duke, our German shepherd, had done his business. I felt the air go out of me. I felt hopeless. I felt that nothing was present in me. Suddenly, I was light as a feather and could have floated upstairs to our old dining room, where the auctioneer went into his call.

Duke had been my dog, bought for my eleventh birthday from a kennel in a town past New Haven. My father and I had driven there to get him. He was to be my responsibility, one I utterly failed to meet. Care for him fell to my mother, and then I went off to prep school. Tied up on the back porch in all weather, Duke grew snarly, but he was really timid and cringed from most contact. He developed arthritis and when brought into the house went right down to the cellar so he wouldn't dirty things. My father liked to brag that Duke was a nice dog with good manners; he'd take your arm off and hand it to you. I thought of this boast now, of how silly it had been for my father to say something so untrue and to continue to say it as if . . . I didn't know what.

The auctioneer sold our house for a pittance. Driving away I wondered where all the money had gone. My father had played his cards close to his vest and committed as little as possible to paper so that what he had done with it could probably never be reconstructed. Some, his enemies first among them, theorized from the start that he had put money in a Swiss bank account for years. Their math told them he could not have earned what he did and borrowed as they'd heard he had and come up with a big goose egg. One man stopped me on the street to tell me that he just knew my father had worn a money belt stuffed with traveler's checks.

My mother hated to hear these theories. She could see herself as a victim, but the thought that my father had left as a rich man made her a fool. If he had left with bags of gold, then he *must* be laughing at her, at all her nagging and lectures when she, shit-for-brains she, thought they were broke. This she could not bear.

The small, spent man I had last seen at the Bridgeport station had not left with any more than he could have scraped together in a few days and those Indian head coins. No one with full pockets wrestles a stove out of the way to hunt for a dropped coin. I never doubted this for an instant. Nor did Peter, who, present through so much of our father's decline into sad fatigue, dismissed out of hand the notion that he had fled to a secret hoard. But there were those who believed it. The other woman, Baghdad . . . a six-figure bank account! It had an appealing logic.

Rumors of my father having left a wealthy man persisted. Some in Trumbull wanted him to be no better than a thief, but a good thief who had worked hand in glove with his girlfriend until they played out the string and took off. If he was a thief then he was not a failure and what he did was the act of the smart man they thought they knew. It was less bewildering to think of him this way than to imagine him a threadbare loser one step ahead of bankruptcy and jail.

A doctor who loathed my father as my father had loathed him, and who lost no love on me, taunted me at a wedding by telling everyone within earshot that my old man had left with his pockets full, I just could not see the truth because, he implied, I probably had something to hide. I ignored him and friends of his came to walk him away, but when I went to leave he followed me to the parking lot. There he caught up with me. He wanted me to admit that I knew he was telling the truth. I told him not to bother me, that I was going home and, finally, that I didn't give a fuck what he thought.

The obscenity outraged him, and he leapt at me. We wrestled, landing inconsequential punches until his wife ran up and grabbed him and then several guests broke us apart. When I had time to think about it, the man's anger at my father and at me seemed greater than it had any right to be. He had not been a close friend of my father's, had never said that he had been taken for a cent. What was he so sore about?

I saw similar anger in others, and it mystified me. It came mostly from family friends, invariably men, who got madder at my father than seemed rational or entirely genuine. Perhaps they had been defrauded and could not bear to say so. They did not offer consolation or help but extended an anger they implied was equal to our own, as if this was the support we needed. Some of this may have come from their total surprise at my father's actions. He had pulled the rug out from under their understanding of how life worked. Doctors, their colleagues, the men they knew, did not do what my father had done, and they hated him for it.

Later I began to explain their anger by the theory that my father had done what they dreamed of doing. His getting away with it had shown them how unwilling they were to act on their fantasies. In the endless talk and speculation that became my father's wake, I developed many such half-baked theories.

A single theory might explain events for others, but my mother and I could not entertain too many, could not stop relentlessly asking why. Peter had none of this. Having survived the years of tumult I had missed, he had no appetite for post-mortems. My mother and I, on the other hand, could not be stopped.

There was the business failure. Obvious. The other woman. Yes. But both seemed the effects of some deeper cause, something that must be there in his past and ours. We remembered his plan for getting elected to Congress. You got a law degree and then went west to settle in the congressional district with the least number of people. There you opened a general store in the county seat and, giving yourself a decade or so, got to know everyone, did favors, gave credit, made your name a household word for honor and integrity. Then you ran for Congress, and after your election you only had to go back to your district when it came time for you to be elected again.

Yes, he believed that there was always an angle and that he could make a killing by taking advantage of it. Others had a license to steal, why couldn't he take one out? Not a criminal certainly, but a cutter of corners who trusted his own judgment above others'. Critically so. A man who thought he could manipulate the Julius Meshbergs and Joe Burkes of this world. A man who knew them as "chooches, donkeys," to be used for his benefit. Julius worked like a packhorse. Joe's gift for gab? Well, my father had them in his pocket.

It wasn't just that my father was wrong about these two men, and that he almost always managed to partner himself with men who had failure written all over them. It was that he believed in luck. All the rich and successful men he knew had nothing on him but luck, and he expected it would come his way. That belief allowed him to throw his enterprises into the air, confident that they would all land heads up. He could say he was never a gambler because he thought he'd never lose. He did not imagine that there were odds against him. Other, dumber, less well-favored men had what they wanted, what could possibly stand in his way?

He was also greedy and, like all greedy people, impatient. He spent the money Julius and Joe were to make for him before they made it, so confident was he that he had a foolproof scheme. He was impatient in another way. The actual details of the schemes he got involved in were beneath him. He could only be the lord and master; he expected his kingdom to be there by fiat, and he expected other men to see in him what he saw in himself. Not exactly crooked, he took the easy way because he believed there had been an easy way for everyone.

As true as all of this might be, it could not satisfy. And what of us? *How could he do what he did to us?* Arrogance and pride, a thousand business failures and humiliations, the love of Gloria — no single factor nor all of them together answered the question that we asked above all others.

One afternoon I sat on my mother's bed going over the same ground we had been over countless times before. Idly, I opened and closed the door of her night table. Looking down I saw cigarette butts, drifting ashes (my mother's lifelong smoking habit has always been a particularly filthy one), and then I spied metal, an ice pick. I pulled open the drawer to find a photograph of my father. He had devil's horns of holes made, I saw, by the ice pick, and a devil's pointed beard. I fished out the mutilated photograph and held it up to my mother.

"Oh, that. I've been doing that at night." She snorted, laughing. "It's a good likeness of the old boy, don't you think?"

I laughed in agreement and put the photograph back in its nest of butts and ashes.

"You know" — my mother sighed — "he left because of you." I bristled at this but said nothing more than "What do you mean?"

"He knew I was crazy about you from the day you were born. That's what I mean. You remember when you came home from prep school how I'd hang on your every word? And he hated that. He would get so jealous. You remember. 'Now that your fair-haired boy is home . . . your number-one son.' You remember him saying that? Of course you do. 'Now that your number-one son . . .' I'm sure that's where all this began."

I remembered, and I remembered that if I wore a hat, the Easter porkpie I wore in a snapshot taken near the forsythia bush in our front yard, my father spoke the lines "He looks like the map of Germany, a real kraut. You put a hat on that kid, and he'll pass for an SS officer." As I walked in front of him I heard him say that I walked like a farmer, a real hick, clump, clump, straddling my rows of corn. My spine curves in and my buttocks thrust out. "You don't drive a spike," he said, "with a tack hammer." When I wolfed my food at meals he turned to my mother. "If he doesn't watch it, he'll weigh three hundred pounds by the time he's twenty-five!"

By the age of twelve I knew that I was not my father's favorite. I could not have pointed to one thing he did or things he did not do that caused me to feel this way, but I knew without knowing why that I stood second to my brother in his affections. I was closer to my mother, a closeness she did everything to encourage, and if I sensed the lack of my father's love, I did not seek it. It wasn't that I felt unloved by him but that when we were together we did not connect. We were an ill fit and could not seem to get along.

The May when I was twelve, my father invited me along on a fishing trip to the Maine woods. He had been going for a few years with several friends to Rainbow Lake, in the shadow of Mount Katahdin, reachable only by a small seaplane. After a daylong drive we flew in over rivers and lakes thick with logs jumbled like pick-up sticks.

We were to spend a week at the fishing camp run by a husband and wife. On the second or third day, my father took me across Rainbow Lake and through the woods on its far side to a smaller lake. We fished it all morning, catching enough trout for dinner and letting others go. After threading our catch on a forked stick, we left them in the lake and went into the woods to have lunch. We walked until we entered a clearing where a flat-topped boulder could serve as a table.

As we ate, my father asked me a few questions about school, standard grown-ups' questions but strange in these circumstances. None of the answers I gave could have been news to him. Then he asked if I had a girlfriend. Instantly I knew what was coming.

He had been playing with a smaller stone, which he now used to draw on the table rock two upside-down *U*'s, one above the other. The bottom *U* stood for the penis, and out of it he had sperm swim in a few wavy lines. This happened when the man put his penis into the *U* that is the woman's vagina. There the sperm meet the woman's eggs, at least some of the time, and a baby could begin. I must not have been giving my father's diagram the attention he needed me to give it. "If you know so much, perhaps you'd like to take over and give me a lesson." He extended the drawing stone to me.

"I haven't said a word. I'm listening. What did I do?"

"You know what you did. It's the way you're acting. No one can tell you a thing. There's no point in me doing this if I have to convince you that I know more than you do. I'm the doctor. Don't you think I know what I'm talking about?"

"But what did I do?"

"Let's just forget about it" — he tossed the rock into the woods — "and you can go through life the smart-ass you are."

"But —"

"No buts! People pay good money to come to me to hear me talk, but I can't get my own son to listen."

"Oh, for Christ's sake what did —"

"For whose sake? Who? You seem to be on pretty familiar terms with our Lord. I don't want to hear it. Let's clean things up and go get the fish. If your mother thinks you need to know anything else, she's welcome to tell you herself. I'm not going to be made a damn fool of." He got to his feet. "What's this? Tears? From a big boy like you? Oh, please."

I didn't want to cry and cursed myself for doing so but silently this time. I *did* want to know about sex. Not the rudiments that I already knew but how did you get a girl to do it? How did it feel? I remembered my father's tongue touching my mother's as they kissed when he left for evening office hours. I wanted to know about that, but I could never ask him to tell me, especially after what had just taken place.

I followed him along the trail determined not to betray my feelings again. We crossed fallen logs. I wanted to pick one of them up and break it over his bald head. At the lake we found our stick stripped of trout by, he thought, a muskrat. I wasn't saying a word. We turned and went glumly through the woods back to our motorboat, then back across Rainbow

Lake in silence to camp, where my father spent the evening drinking and playing cards with his friends.

Mike Cardone, a family friend, an obstetrician and an affectionate man with a silky voice, stopped by with his wife to see my mother. In those early days after my father left, he was one of the few friends to do so. Mike volunteered that my father surely left because of debts. A proud man like your father? Broke and worse? What other explanation is there?

"Your father never, ever should have gone into that construction business. There was no way he could survive that mistake. It was fatal. He didn't know his ass from his elbow. Let me tell you that the first time we came to this house, you'll remember, Patsy, we were standing right here in front of this bar. Well, there were shelves, three or four shelves, there right above it. And full of bottles. Packed." He began to laugh. "Your father fixed us a drink, fixed himself one, and very proud he points to the shelves and tells us he's just built them. The words aren't even out of his mouth when BOOM! the damn things jump off the wall, and there is a helluva crash and a mess. Broken bottles spilling booze all over the floor. We're laughing — right, Patsy? — like crazy, but your father, poor bastard, wasn't. He looked like a man whose best friend had died. You see what I'm saying? He couldn't even hang shelves. How could he get into business with all those houses to sell?" Mike shook his head. "I'll never know why medicine wasn't enough for him."

My father's parting words to Beverly came back again and again to intensify our speculations. As much as we wanted to accept the facts for what they appeared to be, we also wanted to believe that some mysterious force had motivated him.

This force could soothe our guilt over how we knew we had failed him out of ingratitude and distrust, and it could mean that he had not intended to hurt us but had been unable to help himself.

If it was not what it seemed, then no wonder he tearfully asked my mother to let him take photographs of their poodle Apricot. Is that the way a liar or thief acts? Isn't that a man who is reluctant to go, even frightened to leave without taking some token of home, however absurd? But what could this mysterious force have been? Gloria?

We learned that her husband had criminal connections. They had been separated, and she held some incriminating papers, which she used to keep him in line. She had taken these with her. To get them he had to come up with her cut of the convalescent homes they owned together. But what did this tell us? That she had been the one desperate to get out of town? Hardly.

The possibility of life as a bankrupt? Not wanting to face his patients and his friends? Pride. Love. Someone he could start a new life with? Did we really need any more reasons? We came back to these, always a little reluctant to be sure, with a little hope that there might be some other reason to make things come out differently and somehow hurt us less.

Three months after his phone conversation with Beverly, my father sent me a four-page handwritten letter postmarked Baghdad. He had taken pains to print his words legibly. I could read every one, and I did so in mounting disbelief and rage. He blandly repeated his instructions for the sale of the kidney dialysis machine and the disposition of his practice. He imagined these things were already pretty far along, but he wanted to make sure that we followed every step he had outlined. He reassured me that if we handled things properly my mother would be "taken care of." He had not left behind a mess but a well-ordered world. Debts? Not a mention. Gloria? He could have been traveling alone. He used the same calm tone he had used when asking me to wait outside the lawyer's office. The letter ended with two paragraphs telling me about his journey to Baghdad and the wonders he had found there.

I read it a second time, and still could not believe my eyes. How could he? I had Beverly read it. I called my mother, and she too was flabbergasted. What could possibly be the point of his act? We were holding the bag. He must know that. Was he a sadist? Out of his mind? Could he really believe any of this?

He sent Peter a letter as well. Affectionate, jaunty, informative, it was the letter of a traveler writing home about his adventures. He hoped that my brother might come and visit him one day when he got settled. With this letter he sent a heavy silver ring.

In a fury I wrote and rewrote what became a convoluted list of his crimes and cruelties, of his lies and how all of it had caught up with him and fallen on our heads. I wrote a pompous paragraph quoting a stanza or two of Dante's about liars and false counselors. I meant to hurl rhetorical thunderbolts and bring him to his knees if not his senses. It embarrasses me now to think of how windy I was about this. Still, my father would not have had to read between the lines to see how bewildered and hurt I felt. To close, I wrote that I wanted no more letters like the one I had just received. If he wrote again, he had to address the reality of our situation. Who knows what response he had to this? I never heard from him.

In neither our last conversation nor his letter had my father even admitted that he had debts, let alone any obligation to

repay them. For a moment I daydreamed of riding to the res-
cue, doing the manly thing and setting my life aside to do
right by all those my father had betrayed. But I could not stay
long in that cornball daydream. Even if I had not realized
how ludicrous such a thing would be, I really had no clear
idea of exactly who my father owed and only a ballpark figure (somewhere between $500,000 and a million), of how
much he owed. And I knew that his creditors were not raising hell with us.

Yes, the government wanted its money for the back taxes
my father owed — he had not filed for the previous two
years — but my mother sold their split-level ranch house and
this paid those off. John Verdery of Wooster wrote off what
my father owed the school on Peter's tuition; several threatened lawsuits never materialized; collection agencies stopped
calling, and sheriffs had long since ceased coming to the door.

In my daydreams these were the creditors I had searched
out and with a Grade B movie flourish had scoured clean the
family escutcheon. It is difficult for me to believe that I ever
saw myself as my father's son in this way. He had never let me
into his life enough for me to feel responsible, even a little bit,
for anything he had done.

I also daydreamed of going to Baghdad, hunting him
down and hauling him back to face our wrath and justice. But
in 1966 Baghdad was the other end of the world, and I had
no money with which to finance such a hunt. I did report
him to the state medical licensing board for running out on
his patients. I agonized over the letter. Was it right to turn
him in? Deprive him of his livelihood? It was all for nought
as the letter went unanswered. These daydreams passed. I was
left with his past, our life as a family, the very things he had
given up for worthless, to brood about.

And I had my mother, for whose sake I had to attempt to be the man of the family. At first what she needed most was a sympathetic ear. She had "her story" to tell, and she told it to anyone who would listen. She turned the humiliation she so deeply felt into an asset. She talked to the IRS man, the lawyers who called, the banker who visited about her house, patients who stopped her in the street, to everyone she encountered; and to me most of all she poured forth intimate details of her life, of her marriage and of the man who had scorned her.

In doing so she acted in a healthy way. Her refusal to hide anything carried her through the first difficult year after my father's flight. Without in the least meaning to he had freed her from her fear of what others might think of her. She had nothing left to lose and thus, in the phrase of the time that she liked to use, she let it all hang out.

The loss of her house proved to be a blessing. Now she was free to put together whatever life for herself she could. She moved into a Bridgeport apartment and, needing an income, renewed her nurse's license and went back to work. Brave steps to take for a woman who, immediately after my father left, wailed that she did not know how to write a check. In a few years she earned and saved her way to a self-sufficient life.

Through all this, through the boyfriends who came and went, through the friends who dropped her and those who stayed true, and through the painful memories of insult and injury, a streak of pure selfishness sustained her. She was still the "Gimmie–I want–Take me" girl, and the stronger for it. To survive she needed to place herself first, and she never hesitated to do so.

Of the three of us, my brother, who like our father revealed little of his feelings, had the hardest time. He graduated from high school with nothing to do and beat the draft by volunteering for the Army. In Germany he discovered that his black comrades had the drugs he wanted. He buddied up with them, and soon they were all in trouble. Enough trouble so that my brother found he had "volunteered" for duty in Vietnam.

He spent his tour breakfasting on an opium and hashish mixture to get himself in shape for breaking rocks in hundred-degree heat, building an airfield. At night, stoned, he relaxed by watching the light show as magnesium bombs illuminated the jungle on the perimeter of the base. As he prepared to leave Vietnam, it was his bad luck to be caught in a random drug search. The authorities had no trouble finding the tape cassettes he had packed with dope. They slapped him with an Article 15, but somehow (he has always been vague on the details), he got sent stateside, where he was discharged without having to serve time.

In August 1966, a few months before my brother enlisted in the Army, Beverly gave birth to our daughter Marni. My mother came up to help, but after washing half the kitchen floor, she left the rest for Beverly to finish. She spent the week before and after Marni's birth talking. She refined her story and added several flourishes that were irksome to me.

"His leaving me," she might begin, "I can understand that, but you boys? How could he leave you? I know he'll come back to see you, and he'll see Marni too. I know he'll love her."

"Love her? Jesus Christ, Mother, love her? He won't love her because he won't see her. And what makes you think he'll go all mushy and race back to see Peter and me?"

"A mother's instinct." She smiled a sly smile.

"He's *not* coming back. You know it and I know it. You make it sound as if he didn't leave for a reason. Imagine the reception they'll give him in Trumbull when he returns to see his beloved boys."

"Look, he left me, not you. When he was around, you and your brother had it pretty damn good. Don't forget that."

My mother had developed a way of defending my father against my "attacks." I began to see that she felt I had no right to condemn my father. That was her prerogative. It irritated me, but what really got to me was the "love" for Marni and my father's eternal feeling for his sons that she had invented out of whole cloth. My mother got a rise out of me every time. We fought, not in a knock-down-drag-out way, but in flare-ups. What troubled me most was my growing realization that my mother liked picking these fights. She wanted her story to be center stage all the time.

From Hanover we moved to Belmont, and then, when Beverly inherited some money, we bought a house in West Concord, twenty miles outside of Boston. We did this hurriedly and with not a thought about the community in which we proposed to live. Nanny Mench could no longer manage for herself in Pennsylvania, so we needed a place big enough for her. She came to us and stayed four years, increasingly uncomfortable ones for her as well as for us.

My father's leaving had stunned her. She still couldn't quite accept it. "Your grandfather and I always," she repeated, "always thanked our lucky stars that no matter what happened to us our Pats was well taken care of. I'm only grateful that your grandfather's not here to see what your father did. It would have killed him. He would never have understood what's happened to your mother, and I don't either."

She listened to our conversations about my father, but she took little part in them. She had written him off, and when my mother picked up on this attitude it irritated her, and they battled. My mother could not seem to permit any attitude toward my father that she had not sanctioned.

I had begun to transform my father's story into a humorous monologue. Whereas my mother could tell her story to a clerk in the motor vehicles office while applying for a new license, I needed a few drinks in me and an audience of friends. By this time I had written a few poems about my father, but, like most of the poems I wrote then, they lacked shape and force. I could not seem to get my true feelings into them because, in part, I did not seem certain about what these feelings actually were. It was natural for me to act out my confusion as a funny story, to triumph over it in that way, and I had great characters in Joe Burke, Julius Meshberg, Lefty, and Lawyer Adley. Best of all I had my father, the man who once confided in me that Italians are not really white men. I had his waxed mustache and his crude humor. I had heard a bride gasp after he'd said, "You had your honeymoon in Bermuda? Well, that's nice, but it doesn't really matter, does it? All ceilings look alike." There was the Thanksgiving he got us the wrong room in the Hotel McAlpine, from which we could see only a fragment of the Macy's Thanksgiving Day parade. And the night after JFK's assassination when we went with the Adleys to Morey's in New Haven and he gave me hell for wearing a black armband.

Others may have caught the note of desperation in this, Beverly certainly did, but I heard only the laughter of my friends. I got the attention I needed and got the story told in a way that showed me to be superior to its emotional complications. Had I thought that humor was the stake I could plunge into the vampire's heart? Perhaps, but I did not know then of the past's long reach and had no idea that what we were laughing about was far from over.

In six years we had heard little about my father. A former patient who remained a friend of Gloria and Frank passed on what information we had. My Hungarian grandmother had visited the happy couple in Baghdad, and then Gloria had died of cancer. She may have been married to my father, who may have taken advantage of the Muslim dispensation and divorced my mother by looking toward Mecca and repeating three times, "I divorce you." Had my father remained in Baghdad after Gloria's death? We did not know.

In Vermont in the summer of 1971 I began to write my first book about my father, *A Boy and His Dad*. I was now the father of two daughters (Arden having been born in 1969), an English teacher at Emerson College, a published poet who owned a house in Boston's South End and a prose writer, I hoped, equal to the task of mining my father's story for all it was worth. I planned to write a best-seller and show him!

As I wrote I saw myself in a black turtleneck sweater talking through my cigarette smoke on *The Dick Cavett Show*. I dreamt of redeeming my father's failures and paying him back for his desertion by writing a celebrated book telling his story. It seemed to me a story handed to me on a silver platter, served up so that in writing it I could become the writer I so desired to be.

About the past I thought I knew enough, and I did not doubt for a minute that the truth about my father, his self and soul, lived in the collection of facts I remembered. When I began "A Boy and His Dad" I did not imagine my father's sense of his own failure or his fears at having to abandon the life he knew. Nor did I imagine how agitated or serene, anxious or euphoric, he might have felt on his escape from that life. I did not think I had to. The truth is that I was too taken with what I knew, too eager to have all the answers.

I felt confident that my father's was *the* American story of his generation, that he was the embodiment of the drive for wealth at all costs that came out of World War II. I knew this man of Cadillacs and mink coats, the man dreaming real estate sugar plums, the high roller and big spender, as a cliché. I saw this cliché as the center of the book. I expected that in my artful portrayal readers could not help but recognize this American and in so doing shower me with the success I hoped for and needed to prove myself as a writer.

As simple as my task appeared to me, I was inadequate to it from the start. That summer I finished eighty pages. Laboring to develop some sort of form and failing to come up with one, I talked myself into believing that its absence was essential and a strength. I became distracted by present reality, and thought I could put everything and the kitchen sink into the book. Soon I had a mess on my hands.

That July my brother got arrested in a crash pad near Fort Jackson in South Carolina. He had arrived at his old Army base the night before with a kilo of marijuana, and the cops had been tipped off. Peter had called my mother from jail, and she called to tell me of the bust. Peter wanted her to send $1,000 to hire a lawyer. He believed the lawyer could have the charges dismissed as if he had fallen afoul of a speed trap.

My mother wanted to know what she should do. "Send the money at once," I replied. "But if I do will he cut his hair?" she asked. She had no intention of sending the money. Rage at her as I did, I could not change her mind. In the end I had to borrow the money and send it to South Carolina. This took three days.

Released, Peter headed for San Francisco, where, through a childhood friend, he was introduced to the Hare Krishna sect, and soon he became a devotee. I spent the next few days brooding over his arrest and my mother's reaction to it, talking with Beverly about it and trying to shoehorn it into my narrative. The point I felt the episode made was that in my family it had always been damned near impossible to stick to the subject or even to know, at times, what the subject was. The same, of course, could be said of the book I was writing. My brother's present predicament had been obscured by the length of his hair and then whatever strings my mother wanted to attach to helping him. Her demand was obviously blackmail or she really didn't want to help and the issue of hair was just a red herring. I remembered how requests of mine for things much less important than freedom from jail had twisted around to form an issue we had never been able to agree upon. Jail or freedom seemed such a clear-cut choice to me that I could not see how my mother failed to respond with the money.

The issue seemed just as clear-cut for her. She did not want to help a son who would not do what she asked of him. She refused to be forced, as she felt she had so often been with my father, to do something that she believed to be wrong. She felt that she had been asked to accept the consequences of another's acts, and she refused this as well. I got myself hopelessly entangled with her logic and thought I saw that it reflected or embodied my father's logic and shone a light on the past that I was writing about.

Because of a need to find a place for lumps of gristle like this, I pulled and pushed "A Boy and His Dad" every which way. In a year I had three hundred pages, and the book was finished and ready to go into the world, where I expected it to find a home at once. I sent copies to several writer friends and waited for their praise and enthusiastic offers of help. One friend replied with the polite kiss-off "publishable" but not a peep about his own publisher. Another slapped me on the wrist for misusing the word *fluent*. His words stung enough so that I remember them — "You'll never be a writer if you insist on using words incorrectly!" A third friend claimed to like the book, but he failed to suggest his own publisher for it. I had also sent the manuscript to Donald Braider, who passed it on to his publisher, Putnam. They quickly declined. He then sent the book to an agent who had been at Wooster with me. The agent responded by telling me what a sad life I had led and enclosed a copy of *A Daughter of Zion* by Rodello Hunter, a "laugh and cry book about being a Mormon, a personal story of life among the Latter-Day Saints." It was illustrated with line drawings. He thought I could enhance the commercial potential of "A Boy and His Dad" if I wrote it imitating Hunter.

This lack of interest crushed me, but I found I could deflect any criticism by accepting it as true to my original design. When one of the friends I forced the book upon found it disjointed and difficult to follow, I agreed that this was so and part of the plan. Since the experience I wrote about was in flux and remained "up in the air," I wanted, I explained, a certain confusion in the narrative. When another friend complained, "Why am I being told all this? What is the point of the book?" I gave my speech about pointlessness being the point.

I could keep the truth from myself for a time, but in a few months I came to see that my book was worthless. I rounded up the copies that I had sent out and destroyed all of them. I knew I was not through with my father's story, but I did not follow up my botched documentary — this may be the best way to describe "A Boy and His Dad." I did continue to write poems about my father as they came to me. I could not shake the shadow of my absent parent.

Meanwhile my relationship with my mother had become combative. She took what I thought to be innocuous truths about my father for bad-mouthing him, and now leapt to his defense. She insisted on not a revision of the facts so much as a change in emphasis. Now she concentrated on the years before his flight. He had, she argued, only and always wanted the best for us, and I had no right to make him out a complete ogre.

What she meant, she amplified, was the swimming pool, the cars, a prep school education, the European vacation, dinners in New York, closets full of clothes, everything you ever wanted, wonderful Christmases and, her voice rising, she once threw in my face "our thirty-foot living room!" Having had it easy, her theme ran, having benefitted from my father's generosity, how could I be so quick to kick him when he was no longer around to defend himself?

I might have seen that in defending him she was also defending herself, that she perceived the attacks on him as attacks on her. But I hadn't made him leave, I protested. He never said the cars and clothes and years in school were gifts. Weren't they what a father naturally does for his kids? And as for the living room, well, if I was so lucky to have it, maybe she could explain to me why I got thrown out of it if I so much as put my feet up on its hassock.

And as for herself — she ignored me and went on — she had had it pretty good too until, to be fair, only the last two years or so. She began to blame the upheavals of these years on my father's only wanting the best for us. His were not faults of character but, really, a single flaw that had enlarged until it swallowed him. Gloria was easy to explain. Men who lose their bearings turn to other women, too guilty to seek at home the comfort that they know they are unworthy of.

As Marni and Arden got older and understood enough of the family history to know what she was talking about, my mother redoubled her emphasis that my father was a better man than I would ever admit. She considered it her duty to tell her grandchildren the truth that I either had conveniently forgotten or for reasons too dark to speak of had determined to hide. She decried my ingratitude and the exaggerations that she claimed accompanied it.

According to her, the Braiders had poisoned me; reading (she once blamed Samuel Beckett's books) had turned me into someone who imagined the worst of his parents. My mother had always known how to give the needle, to "aggravate" me, and now that I had decided to pay less attention to her, to stay more with the books she saw as conspirators, she went to the needle with increasing regularity. When my mother dangled bait in front of me, I could not help myself and rose to it every time. I did not have the self-control to ignore her.

On her visits to Boston she so spooked me that I disappeared to the homes of my friends or was just "out," leaving her to talk Beverly's ear off and ask, "Why doesn't Bill love me anymore? What does he think I've done to him?" Home, at dinner, prodded to just give her a kiss or show some affection, I pulled away, sullen as any teenager. She could make me act that age and, in doing so, loathe myself for it. Around her I grew giddy and dithered, laughing, into another self. I argued with her and mocked her, giving her all the attention I had given her when I was fourteen, and all the while feeling guilty that I was not a good son to her, could not be the son she wanted me to be. I began to think that in his jealousy of me, the jealousy she had first put in my mind, my father had decided to pay me back. I heard him say, "She wanted you. Fine, now she's yours, and you'll see what I had to put up with all those years."

I disappeared during her visits in order to avoid saying what I felt. I had begun to hate my mother, and to hate myself for the very thought. And I disappeared because, totally unable to keep her from doing or saying whatever she wanted to, I lost control of myself. I could not stand the person I became around her, a person as crude and insensitive as she was to me. I strode out shortly after her arrival because it embarrassed me to have my children see me this way, and I didn't yet know how to explain her, or myself, to them.

One of their responses to all this was to praise me for being so different from my mother and to wonder aloud how, growing up in the house that I had, I had become me. This flattered me, but I knew that I was not as different from my parents as my children wanted to think I was. Through my mother and my obsession with my father, I kept discovering just how much I was their son. I feared I could not be the father my daughters thought me to be because when my mother tipped me off balance with her pinkie I was not the man I thought myself to be. I had had no idea one could stay so vulnerable to parents so long. Because I suffered these torments of youth in my early thirties, they were all the more painful.

In May of 1975, at thirty-three, I had a nervous breakdown that came as a panic attack. It hit on a Friday afternoon in a grade school outside Rochester, New York, where I had been a poet-in-the-schools all week. It began with a terrible hangover that two martinis at lunch did not quiet. I went into the restaurant bathroom and plunged my face into a basin of cold water. When I raised my dripping head to look into the mirror I knew that something had come over me I could not control. I told the teachers who had gathered for my farewell lunch that I felt weird, faint and a little sick to my stomach. I needed to go out and sleep in the car.

I climbed into the backseat and shut my eyes, but the car began to spin. The teachers came, and we drove back to the school. I was grateful for the motion of the car. But once in the school parking lot, I could not find a comfortable position, feared closing my eyes again, and then I had to gasp for breath and for the first time in my life began to hyperventilate. I staggered from the car into the school nurse's office. She summoned my host, who took one look at me and said we ought to go to the hospital. By the time we got there I had nearly crawled out of my skin. Then his car stalled across the street from its entrance and I thought I'd never make it. My legs were giving way. I had no idea who was moving so spastically toward the hospital door.

In the emergency room the doctor looked me over. When I sobbed that all I wanted was to go home to my own big bed he misunderstood me. "Did I know who was in bed with my wife?" No, no, I cried out. My own big bed! But at the same time I was aware that another, saner me looked down on this blubbering wreck. The doctor prescribed Valium, and after taking the pills I sat trembling in a wheelchair as the two halves of me came together again.

Home two days later, I awoke and saw nothing in the mirror. I had disappeared. I ran downstairs, grabbed Beverly, frightening her and babbling my fear. I took a Valium and the crisis passed.

I did not consult a therapist at once or, after the emergency room visit, a doctor, reasoning, as only a doctor's child can, that whatever ailed me would pass of its own accord. Then, as similar episodes followed, I did not seek help for the most pedestrian of reasons. I refused to be less than a man, I told myself, and was determined to handle these upsets myself.

I could not do so. They handled me until, at Beverly's urging, I went to see a psychiatrist. In four or five months of intense sessions, I discovered such obvious truths or they seemed so obvious to me, that I felt a fool for having waited so long to claim my portion of the talking cure.

At first I saw the doctor once a week, and then twice a week. He had an office at our neighborhood health clinic, where, to my delight, the charge was five dollars a visit. When I entered that small room, I must have given off a feral odor, I was that eager to get to the bottom of whatever had caused my panic attacks. I burned through our sessions, talking into being a life I could inspect, analyze and ponder; a version of my life that began to take shape outside me. Between my talk and the doctor's questions, we created what I could think of as a third party in the room, someone I could regard with a hitherto unknown degree of objectivity.

In a rush I began to understand that I had not permitted myself to feel anything other than anger and bewilderment at my father's leaving, that I had never thought it appropriate to miss him or, considering it had been a decade since he'd left, to mourn him. The night before one of our final sessions, I dreamt myself into a heavily curtained room, twilight and earth toned, with a round table in its center. In the folds of the brown drapes that fell to the floor, emanating from them, a presence stirred that I knew to be my father.

As I recounted the dream to Dr. Malamud it hit me that I

had lost my father and that the circumstances of this loss had caused me to deny that I loved him. Love for such a man could only be weakness. I had felt duty bound to return the blows he had given me with hard blows of my own. I had fled from him as surely as he had from me, and become hardened, rigid, until in Rochester I cracked.

This and other revelations came and went off like bombshells. What I learned seems obvious enough to me now, but I did not know then that what I needed was the comfort of the obvious. I had to know and believe that I was not alone, that my tremors and fears were shared by others, that I had lost a father as we all must and that I had denied myself, as so many do, the nourishment of mourning.

I had to learn that if you meet anxiety's demands, anxiety attacks can be the first step to breaking free. You do not so much conquer the fears you have, overwhelm them, as follow them to their source. In my case this path led to the funeral room where the ghost of my father and I recognized, briefly and wordlessly, each other. This encounter was not itself the answer. Instead, I could now accept that there was no one answer, and I could further see that my desire for such an answer, for the all-encompassing truth communicable in clear and simple prose, had led me to avoid the irreducible mystery at the heart of the situation.

A few weeks into our sessions Malamud pointed out that I constantly claimed to have beaten him to the punch. If he noted a connection between one of my dreams and a waking event, I had already seen it. If he suggested I consider the meaning of such and such, I had already done so. I could not be told anything. What was he there for if I already knew it all? I leapt to tell him how right he was and then caught myself and we both had a good laugh.

I admitted to looking out through a sort of iron barrier of attention, protection, perhaps, against going below the surface of things and into painful areas. In most of the instances the doctor spoke of, I had not really considered the connections he proposed, but I could not admit this even within the freedom of our sessions. I *had* to be the kid on whom nothing is lost, the kid who is one step ahead of everyone else and who knows all the answers. I had been this way since my youth, but only now did I begin to see that my powers of attention, real and phony, could betray me. How could I learn anything from my experience if I refused to let myself? I might have sensed the mystery at the heart of why my father had done what he had done, but I knew I was not yet completely ready to give in to it.

Throughout the midseventies we heard nothing of my father, and the world had few reminders of him for us. In class one semester at Emerson, a student looked me over with a knowing eye. She came from Trumbull and let me know that she knew something of my father's history, but beyond admitting that I was indeed his son there was nothing more for me to say. My mother stopped telling her story. It had grown stale for her, and, in any case, no one any longer stopped her on the street to ask about my father. Now and then I wrote a poem about him. These came unbidden, and when they did, I tried to suppress them. If I was to tell even the smallest fragment of this story again, it had to prove its right to exist. I did not hear even a faint voice urging me to return to "A Boy and His Dad."

And then I did.

Since 1970 we had spent all three months of the summer at Beverly's family's place in Greensboro, Vermont. Built to the design of her grandmother Lucy Sprague Mitchell in 1917, the houses sit on a ridge above Caspian Lake. They are clap-board, all the same size and connected to one another by brick paths under covered walkways. Each of the four houses has its own function: study, kitchen house, nursery and, downhill from the others, the summer house. It was in this last that Beverly's parents spent their three-week vacation. During their stays we found ourselves increasingly at odds with them.

We ascribed their fussing at us both to jealousy — our lux-urious three months in Greensboro to their scant three weeks — and to their desire to let us know who was boss. They accused us of not caring about the place, of being un-willing to whistle while we worked when, for example, cleaning dead tree limbs from the forest floor. They gave us orders, and we began to feel we had to be ready for inspec-tion. Every day some small friction made us uncomfortable in their presence. Even though we lived in separate houses, we couldn't seem to keep from rubbing each other the wrong way.

Inevitably, the bad feeling came to a head. It did so the May Beverly told her mother that she planned to return to school to study for her Ed.D. in psychology. This meant, she explained, that she would commute to Greensboro while I spent the summer there with Marni and Arden.

"Why doesn't he do something in Boston, get a job or something? Make some money?" Her mother Marion wanted to know.

To Marion I was an appendage of Beverly. It was unneces-sary to speak directly to me. She took it for granted that Bev-erly either shared her attitude or would not challenge it, and that Beverly would prevail upon me to do what her parents thought I ought to do.

When I heard from Beverly what her mother had said and what she lamely (so I thought) had responded, I felt that Beverly had not stood up for me. I got angry and a fight ensued. I *did* have work, as a writer, work that could benefit from the solitude of Greensboro. Did Beverly take my writing no more seriously than her parents did? They might have zero interest in me, but I did not expect that from my wife. I might have phoned Marion and had it out with her myself, but this was not the way we did things.

Our fight spilled over, as I knew it would, into Beverly's weekly phone conversations with her mother. Now squarely in the middle, Beverly had to take my part against Marion. Things had reached a stalemate when Beverly's father wrote me a letter. He informed me that he could not tolerate me being in Vermont enjoying its pleasures while his daughter stayed behind and labored in sweltering Boston. Every word in the letter seemed unjust to me. In anger I quickly wrote a response and then tore it up. I sat down again and, taking my time, composed a reasoned response, in which, I know, I attempted to make him feel guilty for his stance. Up to this point the quarrel had been carried on with great indirection, and I was too much the coward to do otherwise. I ended with the lofty pledge that if he really felt the way he said he did then, no matter the consequences for me and my family, he wouldn't lay eyes on us in Vermont that summer.

Sprague didn't answer my letter. Beverly and her mother continued the battle over the phone until it became clear that we were not wanted and that no appeal of Beverly's would meet with favor. On Memorial Day we did not pack for Vermont but stayed home as we would through the entire summer.

My revenge against this was to return to the original

injustice, my father's rejection of me, and this time to write "A Boy and His Dad" as a novel. I did not pause to sort out my feelings or examine my motives but began at once, determined to prove myself a writer who could not be ignored by my in-laws. At the same time I would indict them for the Philistine attitudes they shared with my own parents. I had malice on my troubled mind.

If it was hot that summer or otherwise uncomfortable, I did not let it disturb me. Starting on June 5, I wrote hard every day, raising a knob of callus on my middle finger where my pen rested. I finished the book on the Fourth of July and crowed that Independence Day had to be a good omen. I know these dates because the manuscript is in two blue-gray notebooks on the shelf behind me. Looking through these I see that I named my father John and my mother Mary, and that I used a pen with a very fine point to print my letters. They look like tiny stick figures.

I took a few days off, then typed a second draft, my poor typing skills leaving its pages marred by hundreds of errors. When I beheld what I had done I knew at once that it was another dud. Beverly read it and to her credit could find no words of praise equal to her sympathetic questions about why I wanted to go over all that again. My friend Heather Cole gave the book a very careful reading, and in her every encouraging word I could not help but hear how clearly I had failed.

I may have had malice in mind, but I could not distill it into my prose. I wrote the novel the way I had written my angry letter to Sprague. The hurt I felt came first and never approached art. Instead of forging my sword and shield, I had called myself a writer, demanded that I be accepted as one, argued and fought for this, in my own mind at least, and then delivered several hundred lifeless carelessly typed pages.

We eventually reconciled with Beverly's parents, and I mostly kept the story of my father to myself. When making new friends I no longer served up a few tiny morsels of it knowing from experience the proper moment when, tantalized, I could lay out the entire banquet before them. I had used my father's story to draw people to me, to distinguish myself in their eyes, to become special, and now, sick of it all, I decided to stop performing my piece.

Not that my father ever disappeared from "our" house. There I will always be defined, in some sense, by what he did and my reaction to it. All of this past is, of course, as much a part of my children's history as it is of my own. It only required one of their questions or one of my mother's visits to uncover the live wire that runs through all our lives. My father had never done a thing that suggested to me he had an interest in being a grandparent. By virtue of his absence he has possibly played a larger role in Marni and Arden's lives than he could have had he been the most loving of grandpas.

The summer after we did not go to Vermont, I spent six weeks, late May to early July, house-sitting for my friends Rob Brown and Gay Ellis in Sheffield, not far from Greensboro. Sheffield is deeper into the Northeast Kingdom, and Rob and Gay's house, halfway remodeled, stands on a hill far enough outside of town and up a dirt road to feel remote. While there I kept a diary poem, "Runaway Pond." Into this my father unexpectedly entered, not as remembered or imagined but the real man, returned.

On a glorious June morning, the air so alive it tingled, I walked down the driveway to the blacktop where the mailbox stood. The only thoughts in my head had to do with the beautifully arranged curves of the hill landscape down the valley from me and how I might evoke it all. That day I had a letter from my mother, and standing by the mailbox I opened it. I saw the newspaper clipping first. On a torn page from a Eureka, California, weekly paper, my father.

The photograph showed him in a white hospital coat standing on the front lawn of a single-story building the caption identified as the refurbished town medical center. My stolid father stared past the shoulder of a much taller man, selectman or mayor, in the act of turning over the building to the town's new doctor, who, the caption continued, spoke several languages.

My father looked no older than he had the day I had last seen him thirteen years before. I could not detect any gray in his mustache, and his skull was clean shaven. It occurred to me that I had never before seen him wear a hospital coat. Studying the photo I saw that the medical center appeared to be a converted ranch house, and that the man handing my father the keys wore a suit of an old-fashioned cut. The clipping had been folded several different ways. For an instant I thought the photo might have been torn from a twenty-year-old paper. I searched in vain for a story relating to what I saw in the picture.

In her letter my mother revealed that the clipping had reached her from, of all people, Frank's daughter Joycie, our most distant relative. My mother had not seen her since Frank's divorce thirty years ago and could remember only the round face of a blond girl. Joycie had been vacationing near Eureka when she opened the local paper to see William T. Corbett, M.D., the uncle she had not seen since childhood. She knew him instantly. My mother ended with what seemed to be a bland remark, calculated to needle me: "I just thought you might be interested in this."

Interested? I looked again at the photo, hoping to discover some detail I had not seen before, but I only noticed that my father still did not wear glasses. But was that a glasses case in the pocket of his coat? I could not tell. I went to the atlas and found Eureka on the map of California. How had he come to a town so far out in the sticks? He must have impressed them with his "several languages." How many of these could be of use there.

Seeing my father in this photograph, I realized that I had never expected to see him again. It also dawned on me that now he was only a phone call away, a call I knew at once I did not intend to make. I had no desire to talk to him about anything. Well, I did want to know what he had been thinking as we walked to Adley's office, and as he had talked with me the night before, but I could not now imagine words to open a conversation. He could have called me, but he had not nor did I expect him to. Thirteen years of silence had made their point. I called my mother.

"What do you think of that?" She was excited.

"I wonder how he got back here and out there, which from my map seems way the hell out in the boondocks. How long has he been there?"

"I've dialed information, and they have a number for the old boy. Do you want it?"

"No!"

"You don't want to call him? You aren't the least bit interested? After all this time? He is your father, you know."

"Yes, Mother, and he's been a very attentive one."

"Very cute. This is your chance to get back in touch with him. Don't try to tell me you don't want to."

"Don't want to? I feel a helluva lot stronger about it than 'not the least bit interested' or 'don't want to.'"

"Interested?"

"Why would I want to talk to him? What do I have to say? Did you get the loaf of bread and pack of cigarettes we asked for?"

"Yuck, yuck. Not everything's a joke, Bill."

"No, I don't want to talk to him. I'm not the one who left, who went to the end of the goddamned world and in thirteen years hasn't written or called once. He could call me. We could talk about the kidney machine."

"Oh, you're so witty. Well, I plan on giving him a buzz. I'll bet that will shake him up."

"Be my guest. I'm sure the two of you will have a great time reminiscing, sort of an old home week."

In the morning the phone rang. "I called your father last night." She used a coquettish tone.

"You did." She wasn't going to get a rise out of me.

"We had a long talk, and I feel a lot better about things now, better than I have in years. A weight's off my chest. After all, I was married to him for twenty-five years, and most of them were pretty damned good, in case you've forgotten. I told him about you and Peter, Marni and Arden. He seemed eager to have the news."

"Did he say anything about where he's been?"

"The Near East. Travel. He really didn't say. I don't care about that anyway. What's the point in going over all that ancient history?"

"What about when he left? Remember things are not what they seem? Gloria? Where's his mother? How did he manage to get a job as a doctor? What did he put on his résumé, or did he mark off the last thirteen years to his education?"

"I didn't go into any of that, I told you. I told him where I'm living and what I'm doing. He thinks it's great that I'm a nurse and all."

"He won't have to worry about alimony."

"OK, funny boy. I told him he'd be surprised at me, and he agreed that I never could have done what I've done while he was around. I didn't get angry with him. What's the use? It wasn't strange to hear his voice. He sounded like he always did. He said to say hello to you."

"Hello? Well, hello and fuck you to him! Hello? Mother, what the fuck is this? What are you telling me?"

"I'm telling you, trying to get it through your thick skull, that regardless of what you think he's still your father. You will only have one mother and father no matter what you think, and it was your father who said hello to you. I thought you'd want to —"

"Well, hello is not what I want to hear from him. You can call him again and get all the compliments he has to give, but —"

"Oh, so if he gives a compliment that's bad? You couldn't care less that I'm a nurse. You ought to be grateful that I haven't moved in with you. You just don't want to understand a damn thing."

"But that's the man who left you with another woman and who lied to me until I had no idea which way was up. This is not a prince among men we're talking about, but an irresponsible son of a bitch."

"Have I heard it all? Let me know when you're finished so I can hang up."

"Have you called Louis? He'll get a kick out of this one. I'd love to hear what he has to say about this one."

"Bill, fuck you and the horse you rode in on!"

The next morning I threw the clipping away. Now I wish I had kept it. I'm sure there is more in it than I saw that day. We would have little direct word of my father over the next fourteen years. Through Frank we heard of their mother's Hawaiian bus accident and subsequent death in Florida. He passed on the possibility that my father was married to a Vietnamese woman or lived with her and their two children. At any rate, he had been with her at some point. They had met, Frank knew from an unidentified source, while he had worked for Northrup Aircraft in Saudi Arabia. Before or after Eureka? We did not know, and then we heard nothing.

I wrote a few more poems about my father. Not a thought of him had come into my mind in some time, when my antenna picked up from a combination of memory, experience and language the inspiration that returned him to me.

In one poem I worked out the image of my father as rebel. I imagined he had found the conventions of his life empty and their demands intolerable, and so he had rebelled. He had not rebelled against making money, but once he knew that there was no pot of gold for him, he dishonored his marriage and abandoned the family it was his duty to support and protect. When young I had thought I rebelled against him, but my rebellion had been a few baby steps compared with what he had done. The boy outside Adley's law office had bits of breakfast on his bib while inside his old man suavely told the few lies he needed to make clean his escape from all his responsibilities.

I did not stop there. My father had rebelled against the American conventions of money and success by, first, failing to achieve either; then he had refused to accept the consequences. Instead he had written off the whole shebang. I knew that I could not credit him with doing all of this on purpose, but the notion of him as a man estranged from all that he desired and unconsciously in rebellion against what he sought had appeal for me. In my own rebellion I aped the self-destructive behavior of fifties heroes Dean, Parker and Pollock. Never so extreme to be sure, but they had been models. Where my pattern had been predictable, my father had overturned the natural order of father and son and, in the end, usurped my rebelhood. This all seemed far more subtle, and therefore truer, than the one-size-fits-all answers I had earlier formulated.

Another poem recounted our good-bye at the Bridgeport train station. The station itself had long since fallen under the wrecker's ball, and the splintered timbers we had walked across had been replaced by a concrete platform. Perhaps because of all these changes, my memory of what had happened there had remained especially clear — and it had been, after all, the last time I had seen my father. The poem ends with the image of the blood ties that bind father and son slipping away. Upon finishing this poem I felt a sense of release and thought that I had said my last words on the subject.

One morning, coming home from the store with a quart of milk in my hand and a paper under my arm, I stopped for the light and looked across the street at my house. My heart boomed. I felt great joy that it was *my* house. Never to be taken away from me. Not my father's and mother's — was free from them — but mine and Beverly's and Marni's and Arden's.

Some months later I was having a drink with my friend Jane Ruykhaver, who had known me since I was a college freshman, in her family's home in Wellfleet. Did I ever hear from my father, she wanted to know. Not in years, I answered her. Had I ever thought, she asked, that he simply did not love me?

She apologized at once for asking this, but I told her she had no need to. I had never put it so bluntly to myself, but I knew upon hearing her words that they were true. What else could explain why he had treated me as he had and the years of silence that followed? Yes, he had not loved me. To say this to myself, to finally admit it if that was what I was doing, gave me the bittersweet pleasure of a conclusion.

Not that any of this erased the memory of my father or banished the shadow he had cast over Beverly, Marni, Arden and myself. His story had long since become our story. But now it had moved off center stage.

Around this time, the mid-80s, I saw with the sudden force of an insight arrived after long delay, that my father had ceased to be "my subject." My mother had long since been the dominate parent in my life. Even as I pursued my father, it had been my mother, whose brass and sense of humor I had inherited, whose demanding presence I could not free myself from. I felt the shock you feel when you finally see the obvious. In all that I had written about my father I had overlooked my mother's role. How dull of me to think that it had ever been just a boy and his dad!

My parents had in common the sustaining inner resource of pure selfishness. Both of them could turn the world off and guiltlessly go about their own business certain that nothing else mattered. My father did this furtively and avoided explaining himself. My mother had an explanation for everything she did. My father wanted to be offstage, but my mother sought the spotlight.

Arriving at our house my mother always, and I do not exaggerate, left her car running in the middle of the street for me to park and ran through our front door to, she sang out, take a pee. She felt her family ought to wait on her hand and foot, and she saw no reason why this could not start the moment she arrived. After waltzing into Harvard's Peabody Museum and past the admission desk, she threw over her shoulder, "I'm Bill's mother." When I came in the clerk asked me if I was Bill and laughingly collected for my mother as well as me. "Well," my mother huffed when I asked her about this, "I thought that since you teach here they'd know who you are."

And my mother accepted credit for every one of her acts, no matter how outrageous. She proudly explained throwing the dead and frozen body of her poodle Apricot onto the lawn of a Bridgeport funeral parlor: "I had her in the freezer because I didn't know what to do with her, and then I thought I could put her in our Dumpster, but what if someone found her and recognized her and came to the door? So I stuffed her in a pillowcase and rode around town until it hit me that an undertaker would know what to do with a dead body even if it was a dog's."

To my mother these were all comic stories. She could let rip a fart and laugh heartily. No joke was too corny or vulgar for her. This crude vitality never deserted her, but in old age it did not always wear well on others and she began to be laughed at. At a full Thanksgiving table, she asked me if I remembered a man she had appeared in plays with. I did not. She described him, but I still had no idea who she was talking about. She kept after me until she had everyone's attention.

"Bill, are you sure you don't remember him?"

"Absolutely."

"Well, fuck you. He died of cancer."

One Christmas she batted her eyes across the table at Marni's Florentine boyfriend. Gabriele had only just met her and, his English being rudimentary, did not know how to express his bewilderment as she continued to flirt with him. She was not too old to be the life of the party, and if she caused embarrassment or pain, you could not call her on it without getting the retort "I've seen you do worse."

Beverly had long since learned a rhythm of nods, hmms and huhs on which to ride out my mother's monologues without really listening to them. But I heard every word my mother said. I was powerless to keep her from saying and do-ing exactly as she pleased and powerless to ignore whatever she did or said. After one especially trying weekend visit, I had the first panic attack I'd suffered in over a decade.

When she decided to retire from nursing, my mother pressed us about coming to live in Boston. We could, she urged, make the fourth floor of our house over for her, and she'd have an apartment of her own. Over our dead bodies! She must have heard this in something that we said because she turned, without so much as a skirmish, to my brother, who had recently moved from Los Angeles to Provo, Utah. He had opened a vegetarian restaurant and a radio station that broadcast Krishna lectures on vegetarianism twenty-four hours a day. When she visited him she enjoyed herself so much that she moved there forthwith and quickly found a condominium looking toward Mount Timpanogos.

Every significant difference between Connecticut and Utah — climate, topography and the Mormons, in whom she developed an interest — appealed to her. My mother oc-casionally ate at my brother's restaurant, but she did not de-pend on him and his family for her social life. She found this in the community of condos in which she lived, and within weeks she was gambling in Las Vegas and touring Salt Lake City with new friends. It surprised and delighted me, for self-ish reasons, that she found herself so at home in Utah. She even treated herself to a pet, a mutt, part long-haired dachs-hund, that she named Timpy after the mountain she enjoyed viewing from her back porch.

On a June morning, just before dawn, she awoke thirsty, and as she was making her way down the dark stairs for a glass of milk Timpy got entangled in her feet and she tripped. In reaching out to break her fall, she landed on her wrist, and it shattered. She had cracked several ribs as well and lay there for a few hours in intense pain and shock before she could think to crawl to the phone and call Peter. That afternoon he called me in Vermont to tell me her of accident. I called the hospi-tal and spoke to her. Through the painkillers she apologized for falling and hoped that Timpy had not been hurt and would be taken care of by my brother.

Two days later Peter phoned to say that things looked bad. I took this news as if I had expected it. My mother was breath-ing with difficulty. A lifetime cigarette smoker, she had weak lungs to begin with, and now the pain from her cracked ribs prevented her from taking a deep breath. Her lungs were filling up with fluid. Should I come out? My brother thought not.

That night I decided I could not go to her side. I knew I could never say to her what she wanted to hear, could not force myself to offer her the comfort she needed, could not, in short, do my duty. I told my brother this, and Peter sweetly said that it hardly mattered, as she was now mostly out of it. There wasn't a thing I could do for her. But I knew the choice not to go had been mine. My conscience troubled me, but not enough to make me change my mind.

Over the seven days of my mother's dying, I became more and more agitated and eager for it to be over and done with. I could do nothing but wait, and I hated it. Finally, on June 11, Peter called to tell me that she had died that morning. In delirium the night before she had spoken her last words: "How is Bill in Boston?"

Marni was with me. After hearing the news, we walked in the rain to the cemetery where Beverly's father lies buried. We talked of her Nanny Pats and her love for *Forever Amber* and *Gone With the Wind,* for Bette Davis, Lucille Ball and clothes. We laughed over her outrageous behavior. Later we sat before a fire, alternately talking intently and being silent. Marni said she loved her grandmother in spite of everything. Incapable of being the son she had wanted, I, alas, could not say as much.

Over the next few days I called several of my mother's friends, including two women she had known since childhood, and then I called Louis Kaye, to whom I had not spoken in years. Having grown accustomed to death, all of them took the news in stride. I did not cry a tear, but spent many moments that summer looking up from whatever book I was reading to stare out over Caspian Lake and say again to myself that my mother was really dead. Slowly, I began to accept the truth of this.

A few days after she died, I flew to Provo to spend some time helping my brother sort through her things. It had been over twenty years since we had spent more than a few hours together. When we talked about our parents, Peter claimed to have little memory of our growing up. Incident after incident that I remembered clearly he could not recall. What he did remember seemed to arouse little emotion in him. My memories, as well as my memory, perplexed him. I could see that his forgetfulness was, in part, an act of will, but it pained him not to remember. I stopped bringing up our past.

I spent my second morning in Provo alone in my brother's restaurant taking a close look at the box of loose photographs and the few scrapbooks my mother had kept. I sat under my brother's deities, elephant-faced Indian gods absolutely alien to me. There were three scrapbooks. The black pages in two of them were empty except for the stick-on corners that had once held photographs. In the third book my mother had pasted the poems of mine that she'd had published in the *Trumbull Times*. I flipped to the book's title page: "The Literary Works of William T. Corbett, Jr.," my mother had written with a flourish. For the first time in years I read the poems of my youth and saw that they were preoccupied with death. They took up two pages. The hundred and more pages that followed were blank.

I had given my mother my first two or three pamphlets, but she claimed not to understand the poems. For years she had badgered me to write a poem to her. "You can call it 'Poem to Me Mother,'" she said. After she had been in our house, I sometimes found my desk in disarray, and I knew she had been looking through my papers. She could have asked to see my books, but she didn't. I had not showed her anything I had written in over twenty years.

We were not a picture-taking family. My father bought himself a good camera, but he forgot it at home when we went on trips, or the pictures he did take failed to come out right, or our clowning when he tried to get us to pose infuriated him so that he snapped the leather case back over the camera and said to hell with it. I had been the one who usually put a finger up my nose or made the faces that caused my father to blow up.

Now I see my brother and myself dressed like miniature men in identical trench coats and porkpie hats. The forsythia bush behind us is in bloom. It is Easter. I model my Upper Long Hill Indians baseball uniform. (My parents hated how I bugged them to get me to the park early so I could be the first player to arrive.) My brother sits before his lamb-shaped birthday cake, his face smeared with icing. The face that, I remember saying, I hated to see crinkle up: I meant I didn't want to see him cry. There is only one snapshot of my father. He must have just returned from the war. He sits, shirtless, wearing khakis, and I am on his lap.

My mother, I see, loved to be photographed. Many of these pictures are of her by our swimming pool. I have never seen them before. She stands on the diving board wearing a black, one-piece bathing suit, hands on hips, holding the pose of a fashion model. On the back she had written the caption, "40! Can you top this?" She stands smiling out from under a straw picture hat — "Some Kind of Woman." She strikes the pose of an odalisque — "Bombshell." Had my father taken these?

Then I come upon older photographs of my mother and her mother on their tour of Germany, of stout Germans I do not recognize, of my grandmother's brother Al in a silly straw hat and of my grandfather Mench on one knee holding his Scottie dog Jiggs. I come to the bottom of the box and find the white leather-bound album of photographs from my wedding.

When growing up Marni and Arden had pored over these pictures and asked endless questions about everyone in them. I know the book well. My mother's copy shows hard use. The binding is loose, and I open the book carefully. Halfway through, I turn a page and see that the head has been roughly torn off one of the people. It's my headless father dancing with Beverly. The other photographs with him are not in the book. I turn to the last image. Beverly and I are posed between our parents. My mother is next to me and looks glamorous, at her best. I see that she has thrust herself a little bit in front of the rest of us. But I notice this later. My father is not in the picture. He has been cut out. I look closely. My mother must have cut him out with a pair of cuticle scissors.

As I held the album in my hands I began to feel cold, not a chill exactly, and not the cold of winter, but cold from the inside. I closed the album and sat motionless. Emptiness filled me. I remembered what I had felt on the day our house had been auctioned. Anyone touching me would have touched cold marble. The sunny Provo street ran outside the window. I could see it, but I was part of another world, utterly empty and loveless at its core. I could not have pointed to the photograph that triggered my entry into this world, but I knew that my family had never known how to love one another. Did I know how to love? It had been years since I had loved my mother. Had I ever loved my father? I had felt warmth these last few days with my brother, but that feeling sat in my stomach unexpressed.

I love Beverly, Marni, and Arden, I thought to myself, the only family I have, but at the moment they seemed impossibly far away, as much a part of another world as the life-sized, brightly painted Indian gods on the shelf above me. I sat in this cold emptiness for I don't know how long. To passersby I must have looked like a statue. I waited for something to come after the cold emptiness that had overwhelmed me, some revelation. Then I heard my brother and his son come through the restaurant's back door. I left the world I had been in for theirs.

Peter did not want any of the family photographs. He waved them aside. They had no meaning for him, and he would just as soon let me have them or throw them away. I'd take them then. We chatted as he began to lay out the day's lunch, filling steam trays with brown and green food. I wanted to return to the state of emptiness that I had left moments ago. I asked to borrow his car.

I drove from the restaurant into the bare Utah mountains. I had nowhere to go until it occurred to me that I could look for the sculptor Robert Smithson's *Spiral Jetty*. Smithson had had it built into the Great Salt Lake, I remembered, in the late sixties. I drove north to Salt Lake City, where a gas station attendant knew exactly what I was talking about. He thought it had been covered by water. I spent more time in my search, driving but not stopping to inquire. I was really after that state of absolute calm that I had entered in the restaurant. But I could not find it as I drove the empty roads, passing the carcasses of deer, roadkill.

On my last day in Provo, I went with Peter and joined a line of sightseers trudging up Mount Timpanogos. In a plastic Baggie Peter carried our mother's ashes. We reached several likely outcrops from which to scatter them, but climbed on until we found one that allowed us privacy. We stood looking out over the valley that ran north to Salt Lake City. I had never held human ashes before. They were gritty, but after I had let loose my handful into the wind, I wiped an oily residue off on my pants. My brother threw his handful, and we heard, or thought we heard, a tinkle as the wind carried them against the mountain's rock face just below us.

My mother's estate left me $50,000. I had never expected to inherit money from her, and it did not seem rightfully mine. I made no objection to receiving it, but spent it as fast as I could, as if there might be a curse attached to it.

In the weeks after my mother's death I had a few passing thoughts about my father. Was he still alive? In Provo, Peter had asked if I had any objections to his hiring a detective to find him. He didn't know if he'd ever actually do it, but he had heard of people who find persons long missing. I urged him not to. It had been so many years, it had to be clear to him that our father didn't want to be found. It was, but it was equally clear to me that he wanted to do this for reasons of his own, and I left the decision to him.

Two years later the circumstance presented itself and Peter acted. As he weighed leaving Utah and returning to Los Angeles and the mainstream of his faith, he attended a Krishna conference in Hawaii. There, a local devotee mentioned during a coffee break that in his day job he found missing persons. "Can you find my father?" Peter asked. The man said he'd try, and equipped with our father's name and the only fact my brother could supply, that he was a doctor, the man went off. He came back in half an hour. Either there was another Dr. William T. Corbett or our father had kept his membership in the American Medical Association. The devotee handed Peter a San Diego address.

Peter flew there the next morning, rented a car and with the first set of directions given to him found our father's address. It was a modest home in a middle-class neighborhood. Peter rang the doorbell. Nothing. No sign on the lawn or the mailbox and no name on the door. He rang the bell a few more times and still no answer. Peter crossed the street to ask the young black man just getting into his car if Dr. Corbett lived over there. The man thought so, but he was visiting his mother and didn't live in the neighborhood. He had heard his mother talk about him, but he thought that Dr. Corbett might have died. He could not say for certain. Peter's next move was to look for what he called the "Bureau of Vital Statistics" and inquire there. If he actually thought there was such a place, he never found it but instead killed time until he thought he might make another try at our father's house.

This time a Vietnamese in his early twenties opened the door. My brother did not get to ask his question because he saw over the young man's shoulder a large photograph of our white-bearded father.

The polite young man was our father's adopted son. He had an older sister, who was due home soon with their mother. He knew something of our father's other family, but if he had heard Peter's name before he had forgotten it. He did not seem shocked by my brother's sudden appearance at his front door.

Upon arriving, his mother also displayed no shock at meeting Peter. She appeared to be in her late forties and forcefully reminded Peter of the teenage prostitutes he had encountered in Vietnam during the war. This resemblance spooked him. She spoke decent enough English, but Peter's own nervousness and something about her answers made him feel that she did not always understand his questions. She told him the following story.

Before the fall of Saigon she had fled South Vietnam with her two infant children. Her husband either had died in the war or had not survived the North Vietnamese victory. Somehow, she had reached Riyadh, Saudi Arabia, where she had friends or at least someone to welcome her and her children. She had not been there long when she went to the American Air Force hospital with a medical emergency. My father treated her, and then, or shortly thereafter, he asked her for a date. They fell in love and were married, in either Saudi Arabia or, later, California. She called her husband Daddy. They had come to San Diego because of an Air Force colonel or general whom Daddy had worked with in Riyadh. Not long after their arrival they had opened a small restaurant that served Vietnamese and other Asian food. She worked as the hostess, and Daddy did the cooking.

She had loved our father. He had loved her and been a very good father. She emphasized the latter, and both children eagerly agreed. Daddy had died in his sleep of a heart attack between Christmas and New Year's Day in 1989. Perhaps he had died on New Year's Eve. About this she was vague. His ashes sat in the stone urn on their mantlepiece under the photograph of Daddy taken a year or two before his death. He had grown the beard only in the last few years of his life.

She could not remember what details Daddy had told her about his other family, but she knew of his two sons. She did not know their ages nor where they lived nor exactly how Daddy had come to be separated. She had no idea how he had come to be a doctor for the Air Force. He had traveled throughout Asia, at least she was certain that he had often been to Afghanistan and had visited India and possibly lived there. He spoke Arabic and Vietnamese and one of the languages spoken in India.

The restaurant had been her idea. Daddy had become the cook because he no longer wanted to practice medicine. She had never heard of the American Medical Association. Daddy was a good cook, and the restaurant did very well, but they sold it. Too much work. Their money went into real estate, an apartment building and two-family houses. Since they both spoke the language, they rented to newly arrived Vietnamese. They did very well, but then Daddy died and she became so lonely that first their son and then their daughter came back home to live.

When Peter finished, and after he answered my questions

as best he could, he told me that on his way to the airport he had stopped at city hall. There he discovered that our father and his wife owned property valued at between $5 and $6 million. He had thoughts of "going after it" and meant to talk to a Krishna who was a lawyer to see if we had any legal right to the money. I said I wanted no part of it. There seemed no point in bringing down on our father's new family the miseries he had left behind in his old one. We might see some money, I agreed, but nothing good could come of it.

Peter did not agree, nor did he argue. He repeated that he wanted to find out more, would talk to a lawyer, and we left it like that. I asked him to go over a few parts of what he had told me, then said that I would call him the next day to see if he had remembered any more details. Before hanging up he said he had made a date to return to San Diego in a month to spend the weekend.

I called Beverly at once. She could not believe it. Nor could Arden and Marni when I spoke with them. A year earlier Arden had lived in San Diego for six months, not too far, as best we could figure, from her grandfather's house. I had read poetry there in 1988. I reminded all of them that I had always expected news of my father's death to reach us, but who could have imagined it would come as it had. I told them what Peter had said about the money, and what my response had been. In talking to them, such a tumult of thoughts and feelings overwhelmed me that I was not sure what I actually did think or feel. Off the phone, I poured myself a drink. 1988? The first day of 1989 at the latest? My mother was alive then. She could have known of my father's death. Cruel of fate not to let her get the news.

Over the following days Peter and I spoke by phone several times. Now he described my father's wife as small, pretty vivacious and loud. She drove a fairly new Mercedes-Benz. She may have fallen ill after Daddy's death. Peter had the impression that her children had come home for reasons other than her loneliness. He had seen the bed in which Daddy died. Now he remembered a wall of cookbooks, Daddy's cookbooks, hundreds of them, well used. Our father had done all the cooking at home too. This I regretted not being able to tell my mother! How she would have gasped in surprise and pleasure at the news.

About the millions in real estate, Peter had formed the opinion that selling the restaurant and buying real estate had been her idea. But we both could see our father's hand at work in this. Peter had discovered that the properties were in joint tenancy, a term neither of us had heard before. His lawyer would find out what it meant.

I told him that I had changed my mind about "going after it," and that I would go along with whatever he did. It seemed wrong of me not to support Peter if, as heirs, there was money rightfully ours, and wrong to suggest by my disdain that Peter was up to something ignoble. Then too, I had considered the sum of money that might be involved. It might be great enough that I would be a fool to refuse it. Still, the whole business made me uncomfortable. I determined to play a passive role, all the while imagining with relish that a half-million-dollar inheritance would make a final appropriate twist to our father's story.

I am thankful that this twist did not take place. Peter's lawyer soon told him that joint tenancy meant Daddy and his wife owned their property together. At one of their deaths, the survivor was sole heir. Fair enough. Half a million dollars would have burned a hole in my life.

In the fall Peter paid his return visit to San Diego, where

he slept, peacefully, he reported, in Daddy's bed. As he learned more about his father's passion for Asia and his conversion to vegetarianism, Peter knew that their spirits had connected. To acknowledge this connection, Daddy's wife (if he knew her name, Peter never revealed it) gave him Daddy's cane carved with Indian religious symbols.

I was more interested in two other details Peter provided. On this visit he inspected our father's cookbooks. They were clearly the books of a working and devoted cook. And this was the man who in our life had boasted that he could not cook tomato soup, not if you gave him the can, the can opener, the pot and the stove.

To have become a chef, my father had to have become a very different man from the one I had known. I could not see that stiff and formal man serving food to customers, but to imagine it was, as my mother would have said, priceless. Perhaps it is in this collision of images that this book began to grow again. Or in my thought that F. Scott Fitzgerald was wrong when he wrote that "there are no second acts in American life." America *is* a nation of second acts.

And on this last visit, Peter got far enough beyond being unnerved by Daddy's wife to draw her out. She had, she said, loved to dance and have a good time, but Daddy could not enjoy a party. He was a quiet and philosophical man whom she thought of as highly intelligent. She was the wild one in the family. She liked to go out and spend their money. To impress this on Peter, she pulled from her purse a fat roll of hundred-dollar bills and waved it under his nose.

It was only after he left that Peter realized that she had not asked a single question about his life or mine, let alone about our mother. She had insisted he was welcome any time, but he knew he would never return. Would I want to go and see her? I had not the slightest interest. It was obvious that she knew little or nothing about Gloria and the flight to Baghdad. She couldn't possibly know about the last hours my father and I had spent together.

Nor could she say anything to enlighten me about why I had waited like a good boy outside Adley's office door. I had done so because my father asked me to, and after years of berating myself for not knowing better, I now knew that it is easy to deceive those you love, the easiest thing in the world. My father had to get out of town. He had a second act to live, his education to further, and I had been left to find my own way. Daddy's wife could not help me in this.

She did give Peter a copy of our father's will dated 1982. I was surprised to find us listed under section 4 *Estate,* William T. and Peter C. We were far down on the totem pole. If our father's wife Hoa and their children predeceased or died with him, my brother and I, and two sons of Hoa's by what I assume was a previous marriage were to share in the estate equally. The last sentence in the section reads, "The cost of locating William and Peter shall be deducted from their share."